PURE FOOD PROJECT

FOR KIDS!

WHOLE FOOD, REAL FOOD, POWER FOOD FOR KIDS

Lindsay Amilian

CERTIFIED HOLISTIC NUTRITIONIST

Lindsay Amilian

CERTIFIED HOLISTIC NUTRITIONIST

lindsayamilian.com

PURE SWEAT PROJECT, LLC
P.O. Box 30352, Edmond, OK 73003

DEDICATION

This book is a dedication to numerous people in my life, and to those who I may never even meet. This book is not just another project or accomplishment as a Certified Holistic Nutritionist, but it's the outward display of what I've learned as one of the most important components to life as a parent...inspiring and teaching about the importance of nutrition, and how it affects our kids lives here on this earth.

Thank you to my blessing of a husband Matt, who encourages me day in and day out to keep pushing past the challenges it takes to step out in faith and do something that you love.

Thank you to my sweet son Axle, who has been the inspiration in this journey of parenthood. You my sweet boy, have been my grocery shopping buddy, my helper in the kitchen and my adventurous one to try and gobble up every new food that I have put in front of you.

Thank you to my parents who helped build a foundation of healthy foods from a very young age; and without knowing taught me to be content with standing out in the choices we made by showing that our pantry and fridge at home didn't have to look like every other one we may have encountered as a child.

This book is dedicated to all the other fellow parents raising up their kiddos in this journey called parenthood. I pray this book helps inspire and equip you in how to build up healthy and nourished children.

I know and understand how difficult it can be to find the path, and stay the course of keeping nutritious foods and meals going day in and day out.

I hope this book helps give a road map to making mealtime more fun, simple and nutritious for everyone in your family.

CONTENTS

INTRODUCTION

As we look at the trends and the norm of what a "kids meal" looks like in America today, I began to question and dig even deeper as to how this "norm" has become so accepted. Our kids are fed loads of white processed sugar upon waking up with Fruity Pebbles or Cinnamon Toast crunch cereal, donuts, pop tarts, orange juice and maybe a piece of fruit. Their little immune systems are bombarded with a massive amount of sugar, artificial colors and dyes, genetically modified food ingredients and chemicals as they start out their day.

Our American school lunches are sadly a poorly put-together plate of what is cheap and easily made to make in large quantities to be able to freeze and transport to school cafeterias across the U.S. We see processed pizza, frozen chicken nuggets and french fries as the main course for our kids, while they also get choices of chocolate milk and added sugar fruit juices as their drink of choice. What's more alarming is how young these trends begin by incorporating these processed ingredient snacks at even the early ages of 2 and 3 when a child is given group snacks at Mothers Day Out or Preschool.

On average, the majority of American kids don't stand a fighting chance of proper nutrition for the first 10 hours of their day every single week.

91% of American children have poor diets and less than half of that number get 1 hour of daily physical activity. The statistics of childhood obesity continue to rise each year with children ages 2-19 years old according to the National Health and Nutrition Examination Survey. (NHNES)

1 in 3 is overweight, 1 in 12 have food allergies, 1 in 9 have asthma, 1 in 10 have ADHD with the list going on and on. Are there numerous factors contributing to these numbers? Of course. However, we cannot neglect the notion that our current environmental and poor food standards are a direct reflection to our current and rising trends of chronic illness, disorders and poor health in our country.

After all, the U.S. spends more than any other country per person on healthcare, and it is still ranked 37th in overall quality of health for countries best to worst healthcare according to WHO. (World Health Organization)

The U.S. spends more money on healthcare than most other countries, and yet we have the sickest adults and children. We truly have an epidemic in our country whether this sounds dramatic or not.

We see large food corporations making more and more processed foods that are filled with poor genetically modified engineered ingredients like high fructose corn syrup, artificial sweeteners, highly toxic and processed oils, and chemicals that are cheap to make and highly profitable to sell on our grocery store shelves. We naturally have become numb and understandably blind to what it is that is in our food that we eat and feed our kids.

Nutrition is one of the most key essential factors when it comes to not just the immediate visible health of our kids, but it's crucial for their long-term health outcome. I believe so many of us continue to feed and provide certain snacks, drinks and food to our kids that we know is not beneficial to their bodies, but we do so out of convenience, ease, cost, or what we have just "always done."

We may not be able to visibly see what these processed and artificial foods do to the body today or tomorrow, but over the years as our kids develop into adults... I do believe this is where we see huge trends of sickness and disease like obesity, diabetes, autoimmune disorders, food allergies, cardiovascular disease, and neurological disorders that develop into adulthood.

I believe true health starts with pure, raw and real nutrition. While most American children may not start out in this practice, they certainly deserve a chance to start over and change directions. We as parents can begin to re-teach our kids about WHY and HOW nutrition is important, yummy, beneficial AND fun.

My prayer for this book is to be a source of hope, an easy and attainable guide that takes the stress and frustration out of meal planning, a key to understanding of what ingredients are, and what to look out for when shopping for food and making meals. I want the expectation of making a "Pinterest-worthy looking meal" fade away and to make life easier by grabbing more raw fruits and veggies to make up a meal. My intention is to provide knowledge and to stress the importance of how vital it is to protect the health and immune system of our sweet growing babies and kids. I pray it's a source that equips parents to feel confident and comfortable in their decisions not just inside the grocery store, but inside our homes and around our tables.

MEET LINDSAY

I have been a dancer since a young girl and can't remember a year of my life where I wasn't actively involved in classes, competitions, or on a dance team. I was a member of the University of Central Oklahoma's Pom squad and then spent a year on the former Oklahoma City Arena Football Yard Dawgz dance team. After obtaining my Bachelor's degree, I entered corporate America and worked full time in sales as a territory manager for two different large healthcare companies.

During that time I auditioned for a spot on one of the top NBA dance teams! I spent two years dancing for the Oklahoma City Thunder Girls dance team and then transitioned from that to a dance fitness instructor and Certified Holistic Nutritionist. I have been married to my husband Matt for 6 years, and we have a 3 year old son named Axle, and a newborn baby boy named Ridge.

My heart beats for many things...my savior Jesus, my husband and my boys, family and friends. However, being a fitness instructor and helping educate in the topic of nutrition have become deeply imbedded within my DNA.

I'm also an avid researcher and investigator when it comes to ingredients and living out a pure, holistic lifestyle. After battling with stomach issues and inflammation, which turned out to be "leaky gut syndrome," and then a serious bout with "adrenal fatigue syndrome"... I had to learn how to heal my gut, adrenals and my body to restoration. Through this journey, I have tried and tested what it means to eliminate toxins, harmful chemicals and detrimental ingredients from my daily diet and lifestyle.

I am an advocate for choosing organic, non-GMO, and clean ingredient food sources for our family, and want to provide what I have learned throughout the years to you and your family. I'm always being asked about our choices and why we choose them over the conventional way of eating and buying products, which led me to pursue my title as a Certified Holistic Nutritionist.

This book is a direct reflection of the things I've learned in how to shop and prepare healthy meals for kids that are easy and attainable. I pray this provides you with a tool to equip you in the grocery store as well as in the home to feel confident in what you feed your kids to nourish their growing bodies! I believe in feeding our kids TRUE nutrition with quality, clean and pure ingredients without feeling pressured into making Pinterest-worthy meals day after day!

MY GROCERY LIST

I always keep these staples on hand at my house. Having a healthy stocked pantry makes it easy to whip up a healthy meal. I shop at Sprouts, Natural Grocers, or Whole Foods. Check out your local grocery store to see if they carry these brands. I have tried and tested many different products and included my suggestions on this list.

> * Look for items **IN ITALICS**
> They are my personal favorites!

HEALTHY TIPS:

- FRESH OR FROZEN IS BETTER THAN CANNED

- CHOOSE ORGANIC & NON-GMO

- WHEN CHOOSING MEATS:

  - NO NITRATES, ANTIBIOTICS, STEROIDS OR GROWTH HORMONES

  - CHOOSE GRASS-FED, ORGANIC AND GRAIN FREE

VEGGIES

- Broccoli
- Peas
- Spinach
- Green beans
- Carrots
- Red, yellow & orange peppers
- Asparagus
- Celery
- Sweet potatoes
- Tomatoes

FRUITS

- Avocado
- Apples
- Raspberries
- Oranges
- Mango
- Blueberries
- Pineapple
- Blackberries
- Bananas
- Kiwi

COMPLEX CARBOHYDRATES

- Gluten free oatmeal
  (*One Degree sprouted oats, Simple Truth organic instant oatmeal*)
- Gluten free/paleo pancake & waffle mix (*Birch Benders, Namaste*)
- Sprouted or seed bread
  (*Food for Life, One Degree or Dave's Killer Bread*)
- Gluten-free muffins (*Flax 4 life, Simple Mills*)
- Gluten free plant based protein pasta (*POW*)
- Organic pasta (*Rising Moon [found in freezer section]*)
- Pre-made Pizza (*Amy's Kitchen, Caulipower [found in freezer section]*)
- Pizza crust (*Simple Mills, Cali'flour Foods*)
- Tortilla wraps (*Siete grain free tortillas, Nuco coconut wraps*)
- Brown or wild rice
- Quinoa

DAIRY

- **Non-dairy milk, unsweetened almond, cashew, oat, coconut, hemp or pea.** (*Forager, So Delicious almond/coconut blend, New Barn, Ripple, Pacific Organic, Califia*)
- **Ghee or grass-fed butter** (*Vital Farms, 4th and Heart, Kerrygold, Organic Valley*)
- **Yogurt** (*Kite Hill plain unsweetened almond yogurt, Redwood Hill goat yogurt, COYO coconut yogurt, Siggi's Icelandic milk yogurt*)

- **Non-dairy cheese** (*Daiya, Kite Hill almond cheese/cream cheese, or choose options like sheep or goat cheese.*)
- **Organic, non-GMO cheese** (*Rumiano organic grass-fed, Organic Valley grassmilk raw cheddar, Organic Pastures raw cheddar*

**Cow dairy is not my first recommendation as it is one of the top inflammatory foods that causes extra mucus build up within the body and is difficult for the gut to break down and process it. We don't need cow dairy in our diets, but I will list some brands that are cleaner choices IF you still choose to consume it.

PANTRY & SNACKS

- **Nut butter** (*almond or cashew is best*)
- **Gluten free crackers** (*Simple Mills, Back to Nature*)
- **Hummus** (*Lilly's*)
- **Healthy salad dressing** (*Primal Kitchen, Tessemae's, Hilary's, Bragg's*)
- **Ketchup/mustard/BBQ sauce** (*Annie's Naturals, Tessemae's*)
- **Popcorn** (*Buddha Bowl, Boom-chicka-pop, Smart Pop*)
- **Mac n Cheese** (*Annie's organic grass-fed, Daiya for non-dairy option*)

- **Nuts & seeds** (*walnuts, almonds, pumpkin seeds, raisins, cashews*)
- **Snack bars** (*RX for kids, Kize bar, Larabar superfood blend, Larabar Fruits and Greens blend, Wella bar*)
- **Granola** (*One Degree, Purely Elizabeth*)
- **Healthy chips** (*Boulder Canyon, Jackson's Honest*)
- **Cereals** (*Moms Best cereal, One Degree sprouted cereal, Love Grown*)
- **Raw honey or manuka honey**
- **100% organic maple syrup**

GROCERY LIST

PROTEIN

- Black beans
- Garbanzo beans
- Dark kidney beans
- Wild-caught salmon
- Organic nitrate-free chicken sausage
  (*True Story, Applegate Naturals*)
- Organic grass-fed beef
- Organic cage-free, free range eggs
- Bean burritos (*Amy's Kitchen*)
- Frozen veggie burgers (*Hilary's*)

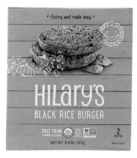

SPICES

- organic Cinnamon
- organic black pepper
- pink himalayan sea salt
- organic lemon pepper seasoning

COOKING OILS

- Unrefined virgin coconut oil
- organic Grapeseed oil
- organic Avocado oil
- organic extra virgin olive oil

PLANT-BASED PROTEIN POWDERS

- *"Amazing Grass KIDS Superfood"* berry blast formula - (1 scoop)
- *"Daily Sunshine"* kid smoothie formula by Beachbody
- *"Dr. Stephen Cabral's Daily nutritional support"* shake (equilibriumnutrition.com)
- *"Garden of Life Raw protein and greens"* (1/2 scoop) vanilla or chocolate
- *"Truvani"* organic chocolate plant based protein powder.
- *"PlantFusion Complete"* plant protein powder (1/2 scoop) - *Vanilla or chocolate*

FOOD STANDARDS

Once you begin to research and understand the difference in how food is made, what ingredients are used and what process the food went through to make it on shelves, the feeling of being overwhelmed will quickly diminish. You will begin to have a standard screening of what to look for when shopping, and you won't be stuck gazing over the labels trying to determine whether it's a quality product or not. Here are the standards of food quality that I look for before I will put it in my shopping cart.

FRESH OR FROZEN IS ALWAYS BETTER THAN CANNED.

If you do buy canned, look for the BPA free lid label.

CHOOSE ORGANIC AND NON GMO PRODUCE.

You can also follow the "Dirty dozen, Clean 15" list that is put out each year showing which foods contain the highest amount of pesticides sprayed onto food, and which foods may contain less. This can be used as a guide on which foods should definitely be purchased as organic, and which ones you may have more leniency to purchase without organic label.

Purchasing organic foods will always be best in my opinion. Our food supply and the soil it is grown in is sprayed heavily with toxic pesticides, herbicides and fungicides that go right into the skin of the food, or directly into the soil its grown into. These chemicals are what we ingest and absorb into our bloodstream as we eat non-organic foods.

Non GMO (genetically modified organisms) labeling should be a big priority for all of us as we grocery shop. GMO foods are basically "man-made" and genetically created. There is nothing "natural" or "wholesome" about GMO foods, and they do cause detrimental harm to our bodies over time.

-"To create GMO foods, heavy metals and viruses must be used to change the genetic material of that original food to manufacture a new man-made one. Literally, GMO foods are "Frankenstein creations" made in a lab by inserting new genes into the DNA of current food crops or even fish....

Additional research is being done right now on their connection to low fertility, gut dysfunction, autoimmune diseases, autism, birth defects and other hormone related maladies." - The Rain Barrel Effect, Dr. Stephen Cabral

CHOOSE ORGANIC MEATS WITH NO NITRATES, ANTIBIOTICS, STEROIDS OR GROWTH HORMONES.

It's also important to choose quality grass-fed, grain free meats that are pasture raised, as opposed to most of our traditional large feed yards that cram animals into tight quarters with poor living conditions resulting in unhealthy meat supply.

CHOOSE WILD CAUGHT FISH INSTEAD OF FARM RAISED.

Farm raised fish are more likely to be given things like steroids or growth hormones to help grow or produce bigger fish for faster turnaround and profit.

5 FOOD GROUP FOCUS

Focus on these 5 categories for
well-balanced, nutritious &
simple meals that will provide fuel
to your little ones body.

VEGETABLES - focus on organic whole food vegetables that are fresh, or second best, frozen.

PROTEIN - this can be organic/non-gmo/nitrate free/grass-fed and grain free animal meat, or plant-based protein foods like beans, brown rice, broccoli, asparagus, nuts & seeds, quinoa, etc.

COMPLEX CARBOHYDRATES - these are foods that are not white, processed or refined. These are energy-producing healthy carbs. Focus on sweet potatoes, brown rice, quinoa, organic gluten free oatmeal and sprouted grain breads.

FRUITS - focus on high antioxidant dark berries & citrus fruits. Blueberries, raspberries, blackberries, dark cherries, oranges, pineapple, mango.

HEALTHY FATS - foods high in omega 3's that provide healthy essential fatty acids to developing brain & eyes. Focus on avocados, hummus, nuts & seeds, wild-caught salmon, Sheep or goat cheese (try to avoid or limit cow dairy), ghee or grass-fed butter, coconut, avocado or olive oils.

5 FOOD GROUP FOCUS

BREAKFAST

BREAKFAST

I grew up in a home with a dad who trained as a triathlete, so our pantry and refrigerator were usually filled with "healthy food." I remember our breakfasts consisting of oatmeal, eggs, toast or even cereals like Raisin Bran and Grape Nuts. My parents didn't buy my brother and I pop tarts, frozen waffles or the sugary cereals like Lucky Charms, Trix and Frosted Flakes that I saw a lot of my friends getting for breakfast. It wasn't the "norm" for me growing up, so I never felt "deprived" or "punished" for not being able to eat those types of foods...we simply did not know anything else and it was normal in our home eating the foods that our parents chose to buy.

I got used to the routine of what my parents bought for groceries, and I think that is how most of us grow up. We begin our foundation of food and relationship to it from a very early age and that foundation is built based on the decisions and choices (or lack of) that are given at such a young age. We may, and often do stray away from things as we grow into adults, but I believe in the idea that a foundation is like concrete and it can be a huge pillar of familiarity to fall back on later in life. I may have strayed into eating whatever I wanted later into my teens and college years, but it's the idea of healthy food as my foundation that I truly feel laid the groundwork to me coming back to the idea that I don't need the processed and sugary foods in my daily routine, so I hope to lay the same foundation for our kids.

Breakfast should be a power-packed meal full of nutrition to fuel our kids bodies. They need nourishment, not loads of sugar that weaken the immune system.

FOCUS ON:

- COMPLEX CARBOHYDRATES
- PROTEIN
- FRUITS/DARK BERRIES

SKIP OUT ON:

- SUGAR-FILLED CEREALS
- DOUGHNUTS
- PASTRIES
- BOXED & MICROWAVED FOODS

OATMEAL + NUTS BOWL

Oatmeal is one of my personal top favorite and highly recommended meals to make for our son in the morning. Oats provide not only a great source of complex carbohydrates, but they also provide protein and have a great source of fiber. Organic gluten free oats are best to use not just for those with true Celiac disease, but for everyone because gluten can create a sensitivity or intolerance for a lot us, affecting gut and brain health. Nuts and seeds also provide numerous nutrients for the body while also giving some crunch and texture to the meal. Ideally, it's best to find an organic, gluten-free oatmeal like the ones listed in my recommended grocery list.

INGREDIENTS:

Gluten-free oatmeal

coconut milk

organic blueberries

sliced almonds

pumpkin seeds

shredded coconut

raw honey

organic cinnamon

Oats are one of the healthiest grains here on earth that also contain vitamins, minerals and a special type of bulk soluble fiber called beta-glucan that helps aid in healthy bowel function, regulation and digestive tract health in the gut. One cup of of oats can equal up to 8 grams of fiber, which is more natural fiber than you will find in a lot of whole foods. Oats are also beneficial with blood flow, regulating cholestrol and supporting a healthy immune system. They have incredible benefits topically for the skin as well, as they help relieve itching and eczema skin type issues.

MUFFIN & EGGS

Eggs provide a load of protein and don't take that long to whip up quickly in a pan! (I prefer ceramic, stainless steel or a cast iron skillet when cooking). If you have a picky eater and they don't like eggs, try sprinkling Cinnamon on top like our son prefers. Flax 4 Life gluten free muffins are really yummy and make for a quick source of complex carbohydrates as well as omega 3's through the flax seed used in the making. Throw on some ghee or grass-fed butter and your kiddos will be sure to love this as part of their morning meal. Raspberries or any dark berries are the best kind of fruit to eat as they are a low glycemic fruit, which means they won't spike the blood sugar and then cause a sugar crash later.

INGREDIENTS:

Scrambled eggs (*our son likes cinnamon on top*)

"*Flax 4 Life*" muffin with ghee butter

organic raspberries

Eggs are considered a complete protein as they contain all nine essential amino acids, (the ones we can't make in our bodies and must get from other foods in our diet.) The egg whites are filled with selenium, vitamin D, B6, B12 and minerals like iron and zinc. The yolk contains cholesterol and more calories and fat but also contains vitamins like A, D, E and K.

CHICKEN SAUSAGE, FRUIT AND MUFFIN

This plate incorporates both fruit, protein and a healthy complex carbohydrate to make a yummy and healthy meal for the kids! It's quick and easy and takes me just under 5 minutes to whip this up. Cook the chicken sausage in either a skillet or a toaster oven, and while those are getting hot you can chop up fruit and put ghee or grass-fed butter on the muffin.

INGREDIENTS:

"*Applegate*" chicken/sage sausage
"*Flax 4 Life*" muffin
blueberries
banana

Choosing a complex carbohydrate, instead of a refined and processed carbohydrate is essential to providing energy to the brain which then transfers it to the body. We want to eliminate white, bleached and processed rolls, muffins, breads, etc and replace them with sprouted, gluten free and whole grain complex carbohydrates. These are the "healthy carbs" that can and should be eaten to build lasting energy throughout the day. "*Flax 4 Life*" gluten free muffins are a great source of complex carbs, and also provide great omega 3 fatty acids within the flax seeds as well. These muffins come already baked in a package of four, so we use about 1/2 a muffin a meal for our 3 year old, but you can certainly use the entire muffin too.

OVERNIGHT OAT JAR

This breakfast meal idea is all about ease and convenience! Simply put the ingredients into a jar and refrigerate overnight to make a filling and nutritious breakfast the next day! For the yogurt portion of this recipe, we like to use Kite Hill's almond milk yogurt, or Siggi's yogurt that contains clean and minimal ingredients. Top these jars with berries, seeds and or nuts. I recommend always using glass over plastic, so stock up on some cheap mason jars and have fun making these at night with your kids!

INGREDIENTS:

gluten free oats

almond/coconut milk

yogurt

*store jar in fridge

IN THE MORNING:

add more milk

berries/fruit

flax & chia seed

Yogurt contains a great source of probiotics needed for healthy gut flora and bacteria. Probiotics are needed for healthy digestion, to help populate the good flora we need to offset bad bacteria which can create inflammation and wreak havoc throughout the entire body. Yogurt helps lower risk of diabetes, colorectal cancer and can boost the immune system. I believe a non-dairy yogurt consisting of either almond or coconut milk is a better choice than traditional cow dairy due to how our cows are raised and the risk of antibiotic, steroid and growth hormones injected into our dairy cows.

AVOCADO MASH TOAST

A combo of protein, healthy fats and complex carbohydrates make this yummy toast a super nutritious way to start out the day. Toast a slice of bread, then spread ghee butter on top. Then mash a ripe avocado on top of the butter and then finish by adding an over easy cooked egg with pepper and pink himalayan sea salt.

Cut into half and send off in hand with kids on the way to school.

INGREDIENTS:

"*Dave's Killer Bread*" (toasted)

ghee butter

mashed ripe avocado

over easy egg

black pepper

pink himalayan sea salt

lemon pepper seasoning

Avocado is one of the best sources of a whole-food healthy fat. It contains fiber, more potassium than a banana, and is loaded with heart-healthy monounsaturated fatty acids.

Avocados can help lower cholesterol and triglyceride levels, and contain 20 different vitamins and minerals which make it one amazing and nutritious fruits to add to your kids diets.

BAKED EGG MUFFINS

These egg muffins are a lifesaver when it comes to saving time in the morning for early grab and go breakfasts. These are a great mix of protein and veggies to power-start the kids day! We really like to add red and yellow peppers, green onion, tomato and spinach. You can also add in some organic chicken sausage and avocado slices to the top. You can bake these the night before, or even on the weekends!

INGREDIENTS:

Egg mixed with a nut milk
Veggies (peppers, tomato, spinach)

DIRECTIONS:

Preheat oven 375°F
Mix up your ingredients and pour into baking cups
OR add some grapeseed or coconut oil to the pan to prevent sticking.
Add veggies (peppers, tomato, spinach)

Bake 25 mins

Eggs are a great source of protein to add in the morning, just be aware if your child has an egg allergy as sometimes they can be a source of allergic reaction in many kids that have been tested before. A great test to ask for if you suspect your child has a food allergy is an IGG test. This is a delayed response antibody test that could reveal if a food group like dairy could cause reaction within the body a day or two after eating the "culprit" food.

Otherwise, eggs are a great option that are filled with Vitamin B2, B6, B12, selenium, Vitamin D, zinc, iron and copper.

PEACH CEREAL

This breakfast idea is similar to cereal, but the primary ingredient is organic granola instead. Fill up a bowl with one of the recommended granola brands off the grocery list (we love "One Degree" the best) and then load up on the cinnamon, nuts, and sliced peaches. Fresh peaches are best, but you could also buy organic frozen sliced peaches and let them dethaw overnight. Top with a nut milk like coconut, almond or cashew milk to make this a stomach-filling meal in the morning!

*You can also choose one of the recommended cereal brands from grocery list if you prefer to sub this out with the granola.

INGREDIENTS:

granola

raisins

walnuts

nut/coconut milk

sliced peach

sprinkled cinnamon

Granola has many nutritional values to it, but one of the best is the boost of fiber it contains. It provides both soluble AND insoluble fiber which helps regulate digestion, and gives bulk and weight to bowel movements making them more solid and easier to pass through the digestive tract. Fiber also aids in release of gastric and digestive juices, making the entire digestive process easier and smoother.

GLUTEN FREE WAFFLE

This gluten free waffle mix with 100% organic maple syrup is the perfect weekend treat! Our family loves to make waffles or pancakes on Saturdays, but we also want to be mindful of what ingredients are used to make our favorite weekend food. Our favorite brands of gluten free mixes are "Namaste" and "Birch Benders" waffle/pancake mix.

*You can also add berries or a nut butter of your choice to add variety.

INGREDIENTS:

gluten free waffle mix
(see grocey list!)
ghee butter
100% organic maple syrup

Use ghee or grass-fed butter and a pure natural 100% organic plain maple syrup. Avoid the traditional syrup brands as they will usually add in more sugar and extra ingredients like corn syrup, artificial flavors, caramel color and preservatives that are toxic to the body.

GLUTEN FREE/PALEO PANCAKES

I often see people posting questions on social media for tips of quick and easy yet nutritious brands of pancake mix for kids. One of the best options we have found so far is an organic, non-gmo pre-mix called, Birch Benders pancake and waffle mix. It is gluten free, paleo and only requires water to mix with the organic brown rice flour formula.

Simply fork stir as much mix and water as needed and make round pancakes on a skillet or pancake griddle. Add ghee or grass-fed butter, dark berries of your choice and top with cinnamon, and an organic pure 100% maple syrup. This is a fast meal to whip up in the mornings and provides a nice complex carbohydrate, fruit with antioxidants and some healthy fats through the ghee/grass-fed butter.

INGREDIENTS:

"Birch Benders" gluten-free & paleo pancake mix

organic raspberries, blueberries and blackberries

ghee butter

100% organic maple syrup

sprinkled cinnamon

Raspberries are a dark berry that is considered a low glycemic fruit that won't spike blood sugar. They contain a great amount of antioxidants, vitamin C, folate, iron, potassium and vitamin E, that can boost the immune system, normalize blood sugar, increase red blood cells and help with anti-aging. They also provide minerals, quercetin and gallic acid that fight against cancer, heart disease, and provide anti-inflammatory properties.

AXLE'S DRAGON SMOOTHIE

What a fun way to get some serious nutrition into our kids growing bodies? This bright pink smoothie is super fun to make and can be made in batches to store in glass jars so you have more for later!

Look for the organic "Pitaya Plus" packs in the freezer section of your local health food grocery store.

INGREDIENTS:

"*PlantFusion*" plant based protein powder in vanilla (1/2 scoop)

Cashew milk (add more or less liquid for thick or thin desired consistency)

organic dragonfruit smoothie pack ("*Pitaya Plus*" packs in freezer section)

Ice

1/2 ripe or frozen banana

organic spinach -handful

Chia seed - 1-2 teaspoons

Almond butter- 1-2 Tablespoons

This "dragon" smoothie is super fun for kids because of the bright pink color that dragonfruit provides when blended up! Pitaya (or dragonfruit) has health benefits like: cancer prevention, anti-aging, immunity and digestion support, etc. This pink exotic fruit is packed with nutrients so it's a fun, yet also super important fruit to incorporate into smoothies.

AXLE'S T-REX SMOOTHIE

How many of us parents could agree that we wish we could get our kids to eat more greens? If we are not filling their plate with other green veggies throughout the day, we could sneak them into a delicious smoothie and give it a fun name like the "T-Rex!" This green smoothie is the secret trick to getting more greens into your child's diet if you have a picky-eater.

This smoothie blend is filled with protein, greens, healthy fats, omega 3 fatty acids and vitamin C. Once it's blended, it makes a nice thick and smooth texture and provides incredible nutrients to the body. Blend all the ingredients up in a high-power blender and you now have one yummy green nutritious meal or snack to place in the hands of your sweet one!

INGREDIENTS:

"Daily Nutritional Support Shake" formula by "Equilibrium Nutrition" (1/2 scoop of vanilla)

unsweetened vanilla Hemp milk

1/2 avocado

spinach

squirt of raw honey

can add chia seeds if desired

Spinach is one of the best "greens" we can consume due to it's high alkaline properties, and numerous vitamins and minerals like: Vitamin K, Vitamin A, Vitamin B2, Vitamin B6, folate, calcium, copper and more. Spinach also provides important electrolytes like potassium and magnesium, which is necessary for maintaining health and mineral loss prevention. Spinach is also one of the best plant-based sources of iron, which is needed to prevent anemia. Choose organic spinach leaves and don't hesitate to throw an entire handful into the smoothie!

AXLE'S BLUE MONSTER SMOOTHIE

The Blue monster smoothie is loaded with antioxidants and power greens by using the "Amazing Grass KIDS berry blast superfood formula. Blueberries are one of the best antioxidant fruits you can give your little ones, they are a low glycemic index fruit with essential vitamins and nutrients to boost the immune system.

If you can't seem to get greens into your little ones diet, adding a big handful of organic spinach is a great way to sneak it in through a smoothie!

*A high power blender works best to create the smoothest texture. We use a "Vitamix" in our home for all smoothies.

Blueberries are high in fiber, Vitamin C, K and B6. They contain folate, potassium, manganese, and packed with tons of antioxidants! They are a low carbohydrate fruit that contains lots of water content, so they are not only nutrient-dense, but very hydrating to the body. The blue color is derived from anthocyanin, a mega-dose antioxidant that is highest in blueberries, making them one of the most nutritious foods to eat!

INGREDIENTS:

"Amazing Grass KIDS berry blast superfood" (1 scoop)

Almond milk

Ice

Frozen organic blueberries

Organic spinach- hand full

1/2 ripe avocado

Almond butter- 1-2 Tablespoons

Cinnamon - 3 dashes

44

AXLE'S BEAR-Y RED SMOOTHIE

Need a way to pack in some nutritious red and dark nutritious colors of the rainbow into your child's diet? This smoothie recipe contains great protein, healthy fats and Anthocyanins to provide some "beary" serious nutrition!

INGREDIENTS:

"PlantFusion Complete Plant Protein" powder (1/2 scoop vanilla)

coconut milk - 8 oz (*more or less liquid depending on desired consistency*)

Ice

ground flax seed - 1/2 Tablespoon

almond butter- 1-2 Tablespoons

frozen organic raspberries

frozen organic blackberries

frozen organic dark cherries

Bears are known for their love of red berries, so what other perfect way to describe this smoothie recipe than to call it "Bear-y Red!" The almond butter provides a great healthy fat, the ground flax seed provides quality omega fatty acids, while the red and dark berries contain an abundance of antioxidants and vitamins! These berries are a low-glycemic fruit, meaning they won't spike blood sugar so don't be afraid to load a hand full of these beauties into the blender.

AXLE'S MUD PIE SMOOTHIE

This smoothie mixture is a perfect cold treat for when our son wants something sweet and fun to eat. The chocolate smoothie is both delicious and healthy, while the added plant-based superfood "cacao nibs" provides a fun dirt-look that contains lots of nutrients too!

INGREDIENTS:

"PlantFusion Complete" **protein powder (1/2 scoop of chocolate)**

oat milk (we use *"Pacific Organic"* non-dairy oat milk)

Ice

1/2 ripe or frozen banana

handful of organic spinach

Top with organic sweet cacao nibs (look for *"Navitas"* or *"Big Tree Farms"* raw sweet cacao nibs)

Using oat milk provides an extra creamy consistency due to how it's made. Oat milk is the result of soaking organic steel cut oats in water, blended at a high velocity and then strained. The result is a super creamy, delicious and dairy-free blend with a subtle hint of sweetness. Out of all the smoothie recipes, using Oat milk in this "Mud Pie" recipe is a must!

LUNCH

Whether you have a toddler at home or a child attending school, we as parents know how daunting the process of prepping lunches can be day after day. The creativity and variety of lunch food can be challenging to a lot of us as we run out of ideas or maybe even get stuck in the same rut of making or packing the same meal over and over for our kids. I remember when I was in school opening up my lunchbox each day and eating about the same 2 to 3 meals that my mom and dad would pack for me. It usually consisted of a mustard and turkey sandwich, or a peanut butter and jelly sandwich with sides of fruit, veggies, chips and occasionally a few Oreo's. As a child, I didn't need some elaborate 4 course meal that never repeated, my parents simply filled a purpose of packing a lunch that met better nutritional values than what the school cafeteria food could provide. I think it's important to remember that the focus of packing a lunch is not to feel like some celebrity chef that never makes the same meal twice. The focus should be to simply give our kids a variety of nutritious food groups to fuel their body, even if that means you find 2-4 healthy menu ideas and rotate them out. These lunch meals provide nutritional value plus fun variety to prevent lunch burnout at home or inside the lunchbox.

Some simple tricks to help keep the morning routine easy if you pack your little ones lunch to-go, is prep some of the meal the night before, and remember to stick to the 5 focus food groups to ensure their nutritional needs are met with the middle meal of the day. Find lunch boxes with plenty of dividers and keep the meal colorful with lots of bright veggies and fruits. Add sauces or dressings listed in my suggested grocery list to use for veggie dipping use!

FOCUS ON:

- VEGGIES
- PROTEIN
- HEALTHY FATS
- FRUITS/NUTS

SKIP OUT ON:

- PRE-PACKAGED FOODS
- DRIVE-THROUGHS

CHICKEN SAUSAGE, VEGGIES & HUMMUS

The easiest way to make a quick kids meal is to find fresh foods visible to the eye in your kitchen, and whip up a plate full of foods that don't necessarily need cooking. Spinach in the fridge, organic kidney beans from a can, slicing up an orange pepper, and cooking an organic chicken sausage for a few minutes takes the guesswork out of meals and makes prep time super simple and easy for parents. Add in some "Simple mills" almond flour crackers for crunch, and you have made a complete meal that provides amazing nutrients to lunchtime!

INGREDIENTS:

Dark Kidney beans are a great choice to add to a meal when you need a protein, but are looking for a plant-based source of protein. These dark beans can provide up to 16 grams of protein per 1 cup serving! Not only are they packed with protein, but they are a great source of complex carbohydrates, and fiber too! Dark kidney beans are also beneficial to helping control blood sugar, lowering cholesterol and preventing certain cancers due to their flavonols, which are phytochemical compounds found in many plant based foods.

"*True Story*" chicken sausage

spinach

hummus

dark kidney beans

orange peppers

apple sauce

"*Simple Mills*" cheddar almond crackers

TURKEY SANDWICH AND YOGURT

A simple, yet nutritious meal that usually takes less than 5 minutes to prepare! Use mustard and Vegenaise on the turkey sandwich as you pick what other toppings you want to add to the sandwich, like spinach or tomato or cheese, etc.

Remember to choose an organic deli turkey that does NOT contain nitrates or preservatives. True Story is a great brand with clean minimal ingredients and does not contain nitrates or any of the junk ingredients that other brands will sneak in.

Adding granola will give an extra crunch to plain yogurt, and you can even top with some hemp hearts sprinkled over the yogurt as well to give an added plant-based protein bonus!

Carrots are considered the veggie to eat for great eye and vision health, so it's one we incorporate a lot into our sons diet. They contain high amounts of beta-carotene (the bright orange pigment) which is then converted into Vitamin A within the body. We need Vitamin A for healthy skin, mucus membranes and a strong immune system. Carrots also contain Vitamins C, A, K and B8, fiber, folate, potassium, iron, copper and manganese (which is important in the formation of bones, connective tissue, blood-clotting factors, metabolism, calcium absorption and blood sugar regulation).

INGREDIENTS:

"True Story" deli turkey sandwich with spinach, mustard and vegenaise

carrots

hummus

"Redwood Hill" peach goat yogurt

"One Degree" granola

CHICKEN SAUSAGE & AVOCADO

One of my most recommended meal tips is to throw the "meal prep" mentality out the window! Sometimes the most nutritious and easiest meals are the ones that are thrown together by simply focusing on the 5 focus food groups listed in my book! Most of the meals I make up for our son are literally what fruits/veggies and foods that I have laying around that catch my eye. This meal is a great combination of an array of foods that provide great nutrition without too much overthinking in the kitchen.

INGREDIENTS:

chicken sausage

avocado

green apple

black beans

sliced almonds

red & orange pepper

hummus

Black beans are not only a great source of plant based protein, but they are a good source of folate and fiber!

Black beans also contain important nutrients like copper, manganese, iron, phosphorus and Vitamin B1, which is also known as Thiamine that is important for proper digestion, memory, energy production and helps with anti-aging properties.

TURKEY ROLLUP

This lunch meal idea gives a spin on the typical turkey sandwich by using a wrap instead of bread! Choose a sprouted wrap that is not filled with harmful extra ingredients like enriched bleached flour, artificial flavors, hydrogenated oils and vegetable shortening. We prefer *"Ezekial"* and *"Siete"* wraps or organic coconut wraps by *"Nuco"* which can be found on *thrivemarket.com.*

INGREDIENTS:

"True Story" turkey deli rollup

"Food For Life Ezekiel" tortilla

"Rumiano's" cheese

mango

spinach

red pepper & hummus

Mangoes are full of beta-carotene which is the brightly colored orange tint found in carrots as well. Beta-carotene can lower risk of developing asthma, as well as boost eye health and protect against age-related macular degeneration. Mangoes are also loaded with Vitamins B6, which is crucial to maintaining healthy brain function and supports healthy sleep patterns and mood health. They also contain antioxidants, iron and up to 40% of your daily requirements for fiber, which prevents constipation and builds a healthy digestive tract.

CASHEW BUTTER & JELLY SANDWICH

Close to the "PB&J," this sandwich could now be called a "CB&J" lunch idea!

Change things up and use a cashew butter, instead of a peanut butter and pair it with an organic jelly like "Crofters" fruit spread jelly which can be found at grocery stores or on *thrivemarket.com*

INGREDIENTS:

cashew butter and jelly sandwich

hummus and carrots

"*Glutino's*" gluten free pretzel sticks

green beans

"*Santa Cruz*" organic apple sauce

"*Made in Nature Figgy Pop*" snack ball

Part of the bean family, the green bean contains high fiber, protein, Vitamins A, C, K, B6, iron, calcium and many other important minerals important for the body to thrive. You can buy fresh organic green beans, or purchase the organic frozen bags and steam them in a steamer basket over stove top for around 10 minutes.

SWEET ITALIAN CHICKEN SAUSAGE WITH VEGGIES/FRUIT

One of the staples we like to use in lunch time meal-making are organic chicken sausages that cook up within minutes in a skillet. They make for a quick lunch idea, paired with veggies and fruit that give a wide variety of nutrition to fuel a child's body all without having to cook a "Pinterest " looking meal!

INGREDIENTS:

"True Story" chicken sausage

red pepper

oranges & blueberries

broccoli

hummus

When looking for a sausage brand at the grocery store, I would recommend choosing an organic chicken source that is non-gmo, does not contain nitrates, and that also does not use any antibiotics, growth hormones or steroids on their chickens. *"True Story"* or *"Applegate"* naturals are great brands that offer numerous flavors and options to switch out each time you shop. Our sons favorites are *"sweet italian"* and *"apple wildflower honey"* in the *"True Story"* chicken sausage brand.

LUNCH

TUNA SALAD

Tuna salad made with clean ingredients for the win! Mix tuna fish (we use albacore white tuna or even sardines) with the non-soy option of "Vegenaise," chopped pickle or capers, red onion, fresh squeezed lemon and lots of lemon pepper seasoning. This makes a nice smooth texture and you can serve by itself, or even put on bread to make a sandwich. This meal can actually serve as either lunch or dinner, so you can make it whenever is best for you and your little ones.

INGREDIENTS:

Tuna salad (vegenaise/pickles/red onion)

banana w/ almond butter

blackberries

cheese slice

"From the Ground Up" cauliflower pretzels

Tuna fish actually has many important nutritional benefits including: the ability to boost the immune system, increase red blood cell count, increase energy and protect against kidney disease, inflammation and cell damage. Not only is tuna packed with protein, but it also contains selenium, iron, magnesium, Vitamin B12 and B6, which a lot of us are deficient in. The most significant benefit is the amount of omega 3 fatty acids, which helps to reduce the inflammatory omega 6 fatty acids that is found in a lot of the processed foods that a majority of people consume.

GRILLED CHEESE SANDWICH

A classic lunch staple that every kid should love! Grilled cheese sandwich using *"Rumiano"* cheese. If you prefer a non-dairy cheese, check out my grocery list for more options. We have found that ghee or grass-fed butter spread on the bread makes this sandwich incredibly delicious and irresistible! Pair it with veggies, hummus and some protein-packed beans and this meal will vanish off the plate!

If you are going to choose a cheese made from cow milk, I highly recommend choosing a cheese that has high standards for quality. Look for a brand that is organic, non-gmo, grass-fed, and states they do NOT use antibiotics, artificial hormones or pesticides in the making of the cheese. Choosing an organic raw and grass-fed cheese from "Organic Pastures" or "Organic Valley" is also another great choice as it retains the natural proteins, enzymes and healthy bacteria that aids in digestion. "Rumiano" is another brand we often buy because they follow all of the above requirements plus, they use organic-approved microbial coagulant instead of animal rennet, making their cheese lacto-vegetarian safe. I personally have a lactose sensitivity and prefer to steer clear of cow dairy, but these selections above are all options that I eat and do not have stomach issues with.

INGREDIENTS:

grilled cheese sandwich made with "Dave's Killer Bread" and "Rumiano" cheese

bean mix of kidney, black and pinto beans

carrots and hummus

LEFTOVER TURKEY LOAF

Leftovers. I'm technically not a fan of them due to possible overgrowth of bacteria that can grow on foods that sit in the refrigerator for days at a time. However, I also hate to see good food go to waste that was cooked the night before, or even day before. Organic ground turkey meat cooked the night before can easily be stored in a glass storage container in the fridge, and be re-heated the next day for a great leftover meal option. Reheat in a skillet over stove top, or pop into the toaster oven for a few minutes to rewarm the meat. To make a fun "loaf" shape for cutting into slices, simply cook your turkey into thick square patties and then slice long for the loaf look.

*Add dipping sauces or a dressing off my grocery list for added flavor!

INGREDIENTS:

leftover skillet turkey loaf

steamed green sweet peas

organic white kidney beans

Siggi's icelandic acai berry yogurt

Simple Mills rosemary and sea salt crackers

White kidney beans are rich in Vitamin B1, which is also known as thiamin, important for formation and operation of brain cells, memory function and cognitive function. They are also full of Vitamin B9, also known as folate, which reduces levels of the amino acid homocysteine in the bloodstream. White kidney beans are high in fiber, cancer-fighting antioxidants and are a great plant-based source of protein!

LUNCH

ALMOND TOAST AND HEMP HEART YOGURT

Lunches don't need to be traditional or boring. You can simply toast up a seeded piece of bread and add a healthy nut butter, almonds and some cinnamon to provide the foundation to a meal. Just this idea alone provides a complex carbohydrate, a healthy fat and protein within the almonds to start the meal off right. Add in some veggies, hummus, fruit and a coconut based yogurt with shelled hemp hearts and you have a fast, nutritious and yummy lunch that is surely to spark some energy in the middle of your child's day!

You can steam or lightly saute your green beans and butternut squash in avocado oil until tender. Add ghee or a grass-fed butter, and seasonings of your choice.

Hemp hearts are a super smart way to get plant based protein into your kids diet. The rich nutty seed contains 10 grams of protein and 10 grams of omega 3 and omega 6 fatty acids per every 3 tbsp! This little secret weapon of ours is used to sprinkle on top of our sons yogurt, cereal, veggies or even sprinkled inside his smoothies! I think it's a great way to add a healthy, clean option of protein, while also giving necessary omega's to your kids diet!

INGREDIENTS:

Toasted bread with almond butter

sliced almonds and cinnamon

Organic green beans

Cubes of butternut squash

"Coyo" coconut yogurt with shelled hemp hearts on top

organic strawberries

carrots and orange pepper

hummus

LUNCH BOX MEALS

Lunch box ideas can be one of the hardest meals to feel like we aren't repeating constantly. As parents, we are trying to come up with new ideas that our kids won't tire from, but yet also keep consistent with what foods will not spoil after sitting out for hours after being packed away. My most often lunchbox ideas still remain plain and simple with a 1) Veggie 2) fruit 3) healthy fat 4) complex carbohydrate and 5) protein

For sandwich ideas: Mix it up with peanut butter, cashew butter, almond butter, deli turkey, tuna fish, or even turkey roll ups. If the deli meats and tuna worry you about sitting out too long, simply pack a small frozen ice pack inside their lunchbox to keep cold.

*For more non-toxic lunchbox brands, see my recommendations in the "Resources" section.

INGREDIENTS:

almond butter and jelly sandwich

carrots

apples

kiwi

"Simple Mills" almond flour crackers

"Simple Mills" chocolate chip cookie

"Made in Nature" figgy pop ball

Kiwi is one of our sons favorite fruits due to its sweet and tangy flavor, but they also have great nutritional benefits to them! Packed with Vitamins like C, K and E, folate, potassium and lots of great antioxidants to keep fighting those free radicals that we don't want in the body. Kiwi is also a great fruit to add for additional fiber to help with constipation.

LUNCH BOX MEALS 2

Another lunch box option for parents who need nutritious ideas to quickly makeup and send off with the kids! This meal includes a great variety of healthy fats, protein, fruits, veggies and complex carbohydrates while also giving a sweet treat with clean ingredients.

INGREDIENTS:

"True Story" turkey deli sandwich made with *"Dave's Killer Bread"* and *"Organic Valley"* raw cheddar with mustard

"Simple Mills" almond crackers

green apple

red pepper

cashews

"emmy's" organic peanut butter coconut cookie

Apples are full of fiber and cancer-fighting antioxidants. They help prevent inflammation, aid in digestion, fight heart disease, and are a great source of Vitamin C. All apples are packed with nutrients, but green apples truly have more health benefits than their red counterparts. Granny Smith apples have a higher nutrient density, so we prefer to buy organic granny smith apples a majority of the time.

LUNCH

LUNCH BOX MEALS 3

This is one lunch idea that often will require a small ice pack on the outside of the lunchbox if you know it will be numerous hours before your child will open it up to eat! Deli turkey sandwiches can be a great way to change things up when you get stuck in a rut with PB&J sandwiches. Just add in some veggies, fruit and a healthy sweet ingredient treat like organic apple sauce and " Hippeas" puffs that are a better alternative to cheese puffs.

INGREDIENTS:

"True Story" **turkey deli sandwich with mustard, vegenaise, and spinach**

blueberries

broccoli

yellow pepper

"Santa Cruz" **organic apple sauce**

"Hippeas" **organic chickpea puffs**

When making a deli sandwich, I highly recommend Vegenaise over traditional Mayonnaise. It's an egg-free like mayo sauce that tastes better and is made with only high quality ingredients and non-gmo expeller-pressed oils, which means they were extracted without chemical solvents. Vegenaise is a heart-healthy vegan option that can replace your mayo jar in the fridge!

LUNCH BOX MEALS 4

A fourth example of a lunchbox idea that could be easily made and stores nicely for the time duration before your kid will eat the meal at lunchtime! Remember to pack a container of dressing, hummus or side sauce if you know your child will more likely eat their veggies if it's included with the meal.

INGREDIENTS:

Almond butter & jelly sandwich

"Annie's" organic snack mix

"Chomperz" seaweed snacks

Blueberries

orange pepper

broccoli

hummus

slice of "Rumiano's" cheese

"Made in Nature" figgy pop snack

This particular lunch idea sneaks in a secret nutrient that most of us are lacking in, which is Selenium! Seaweed is a great source of this selenium, and these seaweed snacks are a perfect way to get this nutrient into our kids diet.

Seaweed contains a great amount of iodine, which most of us as Americans are deficient in or at least low on. We need iodine to make thyroid hormones which control the body's metabolism, and also aids in bone and brain development.

DINNER

Just like many other families, ours too is busy in the evenings when it comes to dinner time. I am a fitness instructor and teach several classes a week during the evening, so I am often either prepping food for my husband and son before I leave, or my hubby is the one to come home from work and get things cooking in the kitchen!

I have found what works best is to focus on the essential 5 focus food groups for meal planning. It takes the stress out of being creative and trying to come up with some elaborate meal each night. After grocery shopping on the weekends, I will plan out dinners with what we have that fits into the protein, complex carbohydrate, fruit, vegetable and healthy fat categories. Instead of feeling like I have to spend hours in the kitchen each day prepping for some elaborately cooked casserole or pan recipe (which is still amazing to do when you have the time!), I simply put together what foods we have on hand that day to fit into my categories.

I truly believe dinner time is best spent around a table where conversation and connection can take place that rarely happens during the morning or into the day when we all go about life. So whether this time is spent at home, together in a restaurant, or transporting the kids around town to practice or games...it's still a time when food can be intentionally thought out, put together and made to be nutritious and fulfilling.

There is something sweet and sacred about the evenings when you can take a deep breath, pause and interact with the ones that make up what you call family. Turn off the tv, put away the phones, or even turn off the music if in route in the car to really engage with your family during this time. Dinner time can be a time where the family unit gets stronger, or it can be used as a weapon to further separate us from our loved ones due to the stress and tug of life's demands and busy schedules. I challenge all of us to make conversational dinners a priority throughout the week, and let it center around the healthy choices we can make through food and nutrition.

I hope these dinner ideas will give ease to your schedule and lives by providing margin on what, and how to cook up some healthy and quick meals for the end of the day.

FOCUS ON:

- VEGGIES
- PROTEIN
- HEALTHY FATS
- COMPLEX CARBOHYDRATES

DINNER TIPS:

- Kids don't need gourmet pinterest-worthy meals, just simple nutritious foods on the plate.
- Dinner should be filled with veggies.
- Look for fresh whole-foods in the fridge or on your counter and make the meal simple.

ASPARAGUS AND SWEET POTATOES

Veggies, fruit, healthy fats, complex carbohydrate AND plant-based protein for dinner! What a powerful dinner to serve up for your little one with all 5 food group categories! To cook your asparagus (which is high in protein) without it becoming soggy, grill in a skillet with some grass fed butter for just about 5-8 minutes.

The sweet potato can be cooked at 400 degrees for an hour to be nice and soft when you cut into it and serve up with cinnamon!

Asparagus is actually a high plant-based protein source. When looking for protein options for your kids, don't forget about the vegetable options that provide plenty of protein per serving. Asparagus contains about 4 grams of protein per 1 cup and is a great source of fiber, folate, Vitamins A, C, E and K. It can help fight cancer cells, helps boost brain function by fighting cognitive decline and is loaded with glutathione, which is an antioxidant to help break down carcinogens and free radicals within the body.

* Ever wonder why eating them can give off a funny urinary smell right after you eat them? Don't worry, it's just the unique sulfuric compound found within the shoots that can temporarily give off a slight smell after metabolized. No reason not to eat this nutritious plant!

INGREDIENTS:

sweet potato with grass-fed butter and a sprinkle of cinnamon

apples & nut butter

grilled asparagus

dark kidney beans

SPAGHETTI

Who doesn't love a family spaghetti night with that rich bold tomato sauce and seasonings? Our family loves pasta night but we cook with a plant-based pasta instead of the traditional white flour pasta. We typically use an organic, low sugar (shoot for under 6 grams per serving), minimal ingredient tomato sauce from our local grocery store. Sauces don't need to be filled with added ingredients, so look for simply tomatoes and seasonings only in the ingredient list. Pair your pasta with some veggies or a salad and dinner is done!

INGREDIENTS:

gluten free, plant based pasta such as red lentil *"Pow"* pasta

organic tomato sauce

avocado

red pepper

grilled chicken

Gluten free, plant based pasta is my #1 recommendation when choosing to buy and cook pasta for the family. Choose to eliminate the white, bleached flour pasta as well as the whole wheat pasta too. There are much better options now with pasta being made from plant sources like lentil beans, quinoa, brown rice, black beans, etc. We absolutely love the "Pow" lentil pasta that not only tastes great, but provides extra protein in each serving. It's a much healthier option to eating carbohydrates, and takes away the guilt of eating traditional white "carbs" with a fun spaghetti night!

TURKEY & PEPPERS

Look for a lean, organic ground turkey brand from your local grocery store. There are many out there, but look for a brand that has a label for "organic, non-gmo, nitrate free, antibiotic and growth hormone free" standards for their turkey. Grill up the turkey into small patties and pair it with "Annie's" ketchup to create a yummy dinner! The combination of fruit, cheese, crackers and peppers will also provide a wide variety of flavors and textures to round out the meal.

INGREDIENTS:

grilled ground turkey

"Annie's" ketchup

"Simple Mills" almond crackers

sliced *"Rumiano's"* cheese

oranges

broccoli & yellow pepper

"Primal Kitchen" honey mustard dressing

Broccoli contains Vitamin K and C, potassium, fiber, folate and is a great source of plant-based protein and carbohydrates. This green vegetable is one of our sons favorite, but we also have learned a little trick to getting him to enjoy it completely raw! We drizzle "Primal kitchen" honey mustard dressing over the broccoli and he will eat up an entire handful of these green nutritious "little trees."

BURRITO DINNER

This dinner idea is one of our quick meal "hacks" in our household. If we need something that is healthy, filling and super tasty to eat, these organic bean burritos from "Amy's" are a lifesaver! They come in the freezer section and can be cooked in the oven or even a toaster oven. They are a great source of protein and come in different options with beans and vegetables or rice and beans, etc. It's a simple main dish course and our entire family loves them!

INGREDIENTS:

"Amy's" organic gluten-free black bean burrito

carrots

spinach artichoke hummus

steamed peas

"Siggi's" yogurt

apple

Peas are technically a fruit since they contain seeds developed from a flower, but none the less they are still a great "green" food to add to your kids plate. They are high in protein, which is why we are seeing more plant-based or vegan protein powders using pea protein in their formulas. Peas are also high in Vitamin K which is essential to help anchor calcium inside the bones and keep them strong. They also include numerous B vitamins, folate, and fiber to help with bowel health and regulation.

*We typically buy organic frozen sweet peas and steam them in a steamer bowl on stove top until soft.

PIZZA AND SALAD

One of our dinner hacks is cooking up a healthy alternative to the typical frozen pizza found in grocery store freezers. We found "Amy's Kitchen" organic spinach and tomato pizza that includes organic, non-dairy, and non-gmo ingredients, with options and flavors in gluten-free too. We also enjoy their pesto sauce and margherita flavors as well.

Add fresh vegetables and spinach to ensure that their body still gets a full array of healthy foods even on these fun family pizza nights!

*Additional recommended pizza crust brands are "Nature's Highlight" and "Caulipower."

INGREDIENTS:

"Amy's Kitchen" organic spinach & tomato pizza (find in freezer section)

Avocado & spinach leaves

raw broccoli

organic tomato

"Primal Kitchen" honey mustard dressing drizzled over all veggies

Tomatoes are a great source of vitamins and minerals that help improve digestion, stimulate blood circulation and help with skin and eye health. They contain a large number of antioxidants that have been proven to fight cancer, which is why introducing them at a young age is important so they grow accustomed to the taste and texture of this nutritious fruit AND vegetable.

*We drizzle one of the dressings listed in the suggested grocery list over tomatoes, along with pepper and pink himalayan sea salt.

MAC N CHEESE AND VEGGIE BURGER

I have yet to meet a child who doesn't love macaroni and cheese, so it would only be natural to include this as a dinner option. However, I am not a fan of "Kraft" or most other traditional boxed macaroni and cheese brands due to the poor quality cheese sources and artificial dyes and preservatives in their ingredients. There are better options out there with cleaner ingredients, which is why when we do a mac n cheese night, we will use "Annie's organic and grass-fed" macaroni and cheese. They use our preferred "Rumiano" grass-fed cheese, and do not include any harmful toxic oils or artificial dyes in their formula.

Pair with organic steamed green peas and garbanzo beans (found in freezer section) along with a veggie burger and this dinner will soon be a favorite meal!

Veggie burgers are a great option not only to use for convenience at meal time, but they also provide a great source of protein. There are numerous brands of pre-made veggie burgers out there, but we prefer "Hilary's" since they provide organic, non-gmo, gluten, dairy, corn and soy free burgers with options like Adzuki bean, hemp and greens, spicy thai, black rice and more.

Remember that not all protein has to come from animal sources, we can aim for more plant-based protein options when we are needing to fill the protein portion of our kids plates.

*Cooking tip: you can place burger inside a skillet over stove top, or for a faster method put the veggie burger in a toaster oven.

INGREDIENTS:

"Annie's" organic and grass-fed mac-n-cheese

green peas

green garbanzo beans

"Hilary's" black rice veggie burger

"Annie's" organic ketchup

PUMPKIN AND WILD RICE

Our son gobbles up this apple and wildflower honey chicken sausage, so we tend to use it throughout the week as an option for his protein source. This meal idea includes plenty of color, textures and nutrition for little ones, so do not be afraid to mix things up even if it is a bunch of random healthy foods put onto a plate.

When buying canned pumpkin, look for an organic option with a BPA-free lid.

INGREDIENTS:

"True Story" apple and wildflower honey chicken sausage

organic canned pumpkin

wild rice

*(we buy *"Lundberg"* wild rice)

blueberries

steamed green beans

Wild rice is a combination of several types of rice, and is classified as a whole grain and healthy complex carbohydrate. It contains more and complete fiber and protein than white rice. Wild rice also has three times more iron, magnesium (known to boost energy), potassium and zinc per serving than white rice. It contains antioxidants to help fight off chronic disease and also is a great source of folate. Wild rice is also naturally gluten free, so it won't affect those with gluten sensitivities or who have Celiac disease.

BEAN CHILI AND VEGGIES

Chili is typically thought of as a "winter" meal, but in fact this hearty protein meal can be a great dish to serve up no matter what season it is. It's a great way to cook a meal when you need a large quantity of food for a large family, or even to take to a party or gathering. I throw all the ingredients into a large pot and add in seasonings of choice like chili powder, black pepper, sea salt, oregano and garlic cloves to spice it up a bit.

INGREDIENTS:

Chili:
Grass fed beef browned in skillet, add tomato sauce or paste, organic canned chili beans, black beans, pinto beans and kidney beans, garlic cloves, black pepper, oregano, chili powder, sea salt

"Organic Pastures" raw shredded cheese

green onion

hummus and carrots

banana slices

spinach with dressing

TIP:
If your little one is like ours and doesn't care much for a soup-like consistency, you can make their own chili mixture by simply using a ground meat of choice and add in the combination of beans, green onions and cheese.

SHRIMP AND QUINOA/MILLET MIX

Need a healthy protein dinner idea? Try grilling up shrimp in a skillet while you steam *"Hilary's herb millet medley"* mix over the stove top! You can buy frozen packages of *"Hilary's"* millet mixes at your local health food grocery store in flavors like Savory mushroom, traditional herb, and fresh greek and golden curry. It makes for a nice side dish and meets a healthy complex carbohydrate food group.

INGREDIENTS:

Grilled wild caught shrimp with pepper and pink sea salt

"Hilary's" traditional herb millet medley (find in freezer section)

steamed broccoli

Shrimp is a great source of protein and easy to grill up quickly! Make sure to choose wild caught, versus farm raised since farm raised may likely have possible growth hormones, antibiotics or other foreign matters given to the shrimp to "plump" them up and quickly sell for profit.

Shrimp contains great amounts of selenium and iodine, which most of us are deficient in so it's a great food to add to our weekly schedule. They also contain high amounts of B12, phosphorous, copper, and choline (a macro nutrient important for liver, nerve and healthy brain function).

GRASS FED BEEF DINNER

We feel so thankful to have found a local organic, grass-fed beef and lamb farm close to where we live. The grain-free meat they provide is not only delicious and smells wonderful when cooking, but we feel good about the quality of what we are consuming knowing it is not a source of added toxins that we are eating for dinner time. You can get creative with how you cook this meal by chopping it up into ground small pieces, or have fun making small patties and adding your favorite sauce or ketchup listed on my recommended grocery list!

Feeding our kids with a healthy organic, grass-fed, non-gmo and grain-free meat can add lots of healthy protein and iron to their diet, but it must come from quality sources that meet the above standards. There are so many toxic substances given to our commercially raised cows, and those growth hormones, antibiotics, and steroids that are injected into the cow are directly absorbed into our bodies once we eat their meat. It's important to find a local farm that you can research in your area, or at least find a source at your local grocery store that has these standards clearly printed on the food label to ensure it is truly a clean, quality meat that will benefit your child, not harm them.

*Because meat and dairy are two of the hardest foods for the gut to process and digest, you can always limit meat to once a week, a few times a week...or whatever you feel is best for your family and your child's gut function.

INGREDIENTS:

organic grass-fed ground beef

raw broccoli

carrots

avocado

black beans

"*Organic Valley*" grassmilk organic cheese slice

"*Simple Mills*" cheddar almond crackers

GRILLED CHICKEN AND ZUCCHINI

Grilled chicken dinners are one of the most common meals for a lot of us, so it's only natural to highlight this menu idea! Find an organic, non-gmo and no antibiotic/steroids/growth hormone source of chicken from your local grocery store, or from a local farm! You can grill it outside during the summer for a fun BBQ night, or simply cook on stove top or bake in oven. Keep your sauces or dressings clean with minimal ingredients, or refer to my personal recommendations on the grocery list to add some flavor or spice to your chicken.

Steam or grill zucchini, and vegetables and pair with a great complex carbohydrate like the sweet potato to make this a delicious traditional meal around the table together as a family!

INGREDIENTS:

Zucchini is a summer squash filled mostly with water, carbohydrates and pectin fiber which is beneficial for cardiovascular and digestive health. It contains Vitamin C and all the great energizing B Vitamins which help support metabolism, and contribute to cognitive health, mood and preventing fatigue.

* You can grill or steam zucchini with the skin still on as the skin contains more of the nutrients. However, if you have a picky eater when it comes to texture, just peel the skin off with a peel slicer.

organic grilled chicken with lemon pepper seasoning and pink sea salt

steamed zucchini

grilled carrots and red pepper

sweet potato with ghee butter and cinnamon

WILD CAUGHT SALMON AND RAVIOLI

Ok, so this may look like more of an adult themed meal, but let me reassure you that just because our kids are younger and smaller than we adults...does not mean we should't feed them the same kinds of nutritious foods and meals that we eat. I know it may seem "crazy" to some to make a meal like this and expect your child to gobble it up, but it can happen when you pair the right seasonings and maybe a yummy sauce to go along with it. If you need to slowly introduce these foods to your little one, start off slow and give small pieces of salmon or asparagus along with something else or mixed into a food they are already used to. Slowly build up to maturing their taste buds by adding more adult-like foods like this and eventually I hope they will be open to eating delicious and super healthy meals like this!

*We broil our wild caught salmon on high for 8-9 minutes in the oven, and saute our asparagus in a skillet with grass fed butter and grapeseed oil for about 5-7 minutes or until tender.

Wild caught salmon is one of the best sources of omega 3 fatty acids, EPA and DHA. These omega 3's are highly important in eye and brain development and function. Omega 3 fats are also considered "essential" meaning you must acquire them through the diet since our body does not naturally create these important fatty acids. Salmon is high in protein, and packed with B vitamins, selenium, potassium and contains antioxidants to help fight free radicals. It's also an amazing food to eat for skin and hair health, as well as fighting inflammation within the body.

*Make sure to choose wild caught as opposed to farm raised due to the risk of having a higher probability of possible antibiotics, growth hormones or steroids, etc given to farm raised fish.

INGREDIENTS

Wild caught broiled salmon with dill, lemon pepper seasoning and pink sea salt

Sauteed asparagus in grass-fed butter with lemon pepper seasoning

"Rising Moon" organic butternut squash ravioli

Basil pesto sauce

SNACKS & SWEETS

"Mommy, I'm hungry!"

I usually hear these words around 10am and 4pm each day, followed by the sound of what could be a small animal scavenging our pantry at home. Our little 3 year old has learned to climb the shelves in our pantry to the top shelf where he knows most of our snacks are kept. I can only imagine what snack time will look like when he is a teenager in the future...but for now, I'll keep cherishing these memories I'm building of watching our little spider monkey scale the pantry shelves each day.

Snack time can be either super easy or super stressful for some parents depending on how your typical day goes. Some parents can easily whip up a healthy snack, while others can get frustrated with the lack of ideas so we end up caving and doing a fast pantry raid of what's visible. Snacks can easily turn into a time of simply satisfying an instant hunger no matter the cost, which may be empty calories, a load of sugar or something else that serves no nutritional purpose in fueling our kids bodies in a time of hunger.

I need to be super clear here that I truly believe we have a sugar addiction epidemic here in our country when it comes to our kids. They are given an overload of processed sugar and dyes with foods, sweets and drinks. I fear we are creating a scary future for our kids not only now, but as they grow into adults. This section of the book is not intended to promote more processed or sugary foods, but to give options and brands of snacks and sweets that provide better alternative ingredients when you do choose to give your kids these types of snacks.

After all, I believe there are some really great ideas here that are easy, delicious and yet serve a great purpose of fueling our kids bodies with nutrition that will keep them energized, happy and full. Snack time is still a time to provide substance to a body that needs fuel to keep trucking along...and we as parents have the ability to make that substance useful and beneficial, or empty and harmful.

APPLE BUTTER SANDWICH

A perfect combination of protein, fiber and sweetness! This apple snack is one of our sons favorite afternoon snacks, and would make for a great after-school energy boost for kids. Use an apple core slicer to cut out the middle and slice the apple pieces thin to make the sandwich easier to eat.

Cut your apple into thin slices and spread a nut butter of choice (peanut, almond, cashew, etc) onto the apple, and then add sliced almonds, dried cranberries, ground flax seed or chia seed and finish off with sprinkled organic cinnamon. Yummy!

INGREDIENTS:

organic granny smith apple

almond butter

sliced almonds

dried unsweetened cranberries

shaved coconut

sprinkled cinnamon on top

Almond butter is a great healthy fat and a perfect choice for a nut butter. Almonds contain antioxidants, Vitamin E and Magnesium which is needed for promoting blood flow, oxygen and nutrients within the body through good heart health and blood pressure!

BERRIES BOWL

What better way to treat your kids to a snack then with wholesome, naturally-sweet dark berries? A small bowl of dark berries is a great snack or treat because dark berries are filled with antioxidants and they also are a low glycemic index rated food so these fruits wont spike the blood sugar or cause a sugar crash later.

INGREDIENTS:

Dark berry bowl could consist of dark cherries, blueberries, blackberries, raspberries, cranberries, and acai berries.

You can even throw in a few strawberries as well to add variety in color and sweetness, but just know they contain a bit higher natural sugars than the darker berries listed above.

The goodness of what grows from the earth will always be my top recommended foods before any processed or packaged foods. So this bowl of goodness is a great top choice for an afternoon snack.

*Remember to choose organic fruits, or to follow the "2018 Dirty Dozen, clean 15" list for which fruits are essential to buy organic.

CELERY AND NUT BUTTER LOGS

Ants, bugs and snow, Oh My!

These fun snacks are packed with nutrition and provide a fun snack time idea to let your kids help create what items they want on their logs.

INGREDIENTS:

Wash and chop up celery stalks into small to medium pieces

Add a nut butter like almond, cashew or peanut butter

Top with sunflower seeds (bugs), chia seeds (black ants), coconut shavings (snow), and dried cranberries (red ants).

Celery provides great hydration, the nut butter provides a healthy fat and the seeds and toppings add bonus nutrients like omega 3's, Vitamin E, Vitamin B1, Vitamin C, Copper and Fiber.

SNACKS & SWEETS

HEALTHY SNACK BOWL

Sometimes for a snack we simply throw a bunch of healthy yummy foods into a bowl and make it like a mini meal. This snack bowl meets every single 5 focus food groups by providing a fruit, veggie, complex carbohydrate, protein and healthy fat! Remember to keep snacks healthy by taking out the guess work and simply add things that can be can be cut up and thrown into a bowl.

INGREDIENTS:

carrots

hummus

avocado

apple

"Rumiano" cheese

"True Story" deli turkey

"Back to Nature" organic rosemary & olive oil crackers

Hummus is a great source of protein as it comes from garbanzo or chickpea beans. These beans are a great source of molybdenum and manganese, while also being a good source of iron, fiber, zinc, phosphorus and protein! Choose a brand that is organic and non-gmo when buying from your local grocery store.

*You can also make your own hummus by blending garbanzo beans, olive oil, garlic salt and pink himalayan sea salt in a food processor until a smooth creamy texture is achieved.

SNACKS & SWEETS

ACAI BOWL

Instead of a smoothie, try this Acai bowl as a fun and nutritious "smoothie-like" snack with loads of nutrition! You can make this snack a project that you do with your child by giving them options of what to top their bowl with.

INGREDIENTS:

We personally love dark berries, banana, coconut, goji berries, granola, chia seeds and pumpkin seeds. Just run your frozen "*Sambazon*" acai pack under warm water for a minute or so to soften, then dump in a high power blender with coconut water and 1/2 a banana to make a smooth blend to pour into a bowl before you add your toppings!

ACAI BERRIES

These berries are a brazilian superfruit packed with nutrients and trace minerals like chromium, zinc, iron, potassium, magnesium, etc. One of the most powerful health benefits of acai berries are the "anthocyanins" which give the berries their deep purple color and act as a super antioxidant in the body. They contain healthy fats and a low amount of sugar, making them a low glycemic index rated fruit that won't spike blood sugar.

SNACK BALLS

Be careful, these tasty snack balls will go fast once you make and refrigerate them!

This is a great homemade recipe to do with your kids that includes delicious, filling and nutritious ingredients that taste close to cold cookie dough. A great after school or anytime snack idea!

INGREDIENTS:

1 cup gluten free organic dry oats.

1/2 cup cacao chips (or dark chocolate chips)

1/2 cup nut butter (almond, cashew, peanut)

1/2 cup shredded or shaved coconut

1/2 cup organic ground flaxseed

1/2 cup chia seed

1/3 cup raw honey

1 teaspoon vanilla

Flax seed is filled with Omega 3 fatty acids, and healthy poly unsaturated fatty acids. These are so important to the brain and eye health of a child, as well as skin and hair health. They are filled with antioxidants and fiber to aid in nutrient absorption and support colon detoxification.

*Choose an organic, full spectrum ground flax seed for this recipe

YOGURT CUP

This is another super easy snack idea that is simple to make and is filling for hungry bellies! Pick a yogurt off my recommended grocery list, and then select what fruits you prefer to put on top of the granola. We prefer dark berries, but you can get creative with this and add in banana, kiwi, oranges, apples or whatever is ripe and in season!

Sprinkle hemp hearts (a great source of plant based protein) on top and drizzle organic raw honey or even some cinnamon on top.

INGREDIENTS:

"*Kite Hill*" plain unsweetened almond milk yogurt

"*One Degree*" honey hemp sprouted oat granola

dark berries (raspberries, blueberries, strawberries in pic)

Hemp hearts sprinkled on top of fruit

raw organic honey drizzled over top

Snacking still serves a purpose, and this yogurt cup provides great purpose when you need something fast after school, or even in a to-go cup for the road.

*Remember to choose organic fruits, or to follow the "2018 Dirty Dozen, clean 15" list for which fruits are essential to buy organic.

SNACKS & SWEETS

POPSICLES

MAKE YOUR OWN HOMEMADE POPS: YOGURT AND FRUIT POPSICLES

You can make your own homemade popsicles by picking a yogurt from my recommended grocery list and frozen organic fruits of your choice. You could also use fresh fruits as they are easier to mix for a more blended look. Place yogurt, frozen fruit or fresh fruit into a food processor and drizzle a small amount of organic raw honey, or 100% organic maple syrup over the mixture. Mix ingredients to desired consistency and then place into popsicle molds with a popsicle stick in the middle to freeze overnight! You can also leave room at top to fill with a little granola for an added crunch.

INGREDIENTS:

*Our favorite blend :
"COYO" vanilla bean coconut yogurt
Organic raw honey
Frozen organic blackberries
Frozen organic dark cherries

STORE-BOUGHT VERSION

"Modern Pop" popsicles

One of our favorite brands to buy is Modern Pop, because they only contain 4 ingredients that are non-gmo! Perfect for a hot summer day, these pops are made with whole real fruit like strawberries, mango, pineapple, raspberries, water, organic agave and lime juice.

*No added chemicals, artificial flavors/ colors or highly processed ingredients like high fructose corn syrup.

ADDITIONAL SNACK OPTIONS

Popcorn

(*Buddha Bowl, Smart Pop, Boom Chicka Pop*)

Popcorn makes for a great snack, but make sure it's a quality bagged popcorn brand, or organic kernels that you can pop on your own over the stove top. Microwave bagged popcorn is usually already pre-filled with artificial butters, added corn syrups, hydrogenated oils and trans fatty acids. (If buying microwave popcorn, make sure ingredients are plain and simple organic kernels.)

For bagged popcorn, our family loves Buddha Bowl organic popcorn that is made with coconut oil and Himalayan pink salt. Secondly, we like Smart Pop and Boom Chicka Pop for quality standards of being non-gmo, and containing no high fructose corn syrup or trans fat.

"Kind fruit bites" **snack bites**

These snack bites do not contain any added sugar and are not made with genetically engineered ingredients (Gmo's)! Clean ingredients of pure fruits without using juices, purees, concentrates, or preservatives.

*Makes for a great lunchbox snack or afternoon snack on the go!

"Hail Merry" **Coconut oil tarts**

Oh my goodness, I can't describe how much we love this treat! These dairy free, gluten free and non-gmo small tarts are made with the cleanest
ingredients like virgin coconut oil and healthy good fats from nuts. They are perfect for sharing by cutting it into small pieces for many people in the family to enjoy.

They come in flavors like lemon, dark chocolate, chocolate almond butter, coconut vanilla cream and also come packaged in "bite" size balls as well. It's the perfect thing to indulge in when you get a sweet tooth.

Candy

(*Surf Sweets, Yum Earth, Torie and Howard, Justin's, Unreal*)

Whether its a holiday, birthday party favor bag, social gathering or a sweet afternoon special treat... candy and sweets have become a part of these celebrations. I believe that we can still partake and have fun with these occasions IF we choose better ingredient options of these sweet treats. We can still enjoy chocolate, jelly beans, a sucker, or some fruit chews but why not choose the brands that offer them without artificial colors, flavors, preservatives, gluten, GMO's, corn syrup or additives.

We as parents know that candy and treats will pop up in our kids lives through all different functions and gatherings as they grow up, so why not find the brands that offer better alternatives to the traditional candies that are filled with harmful dyes, chemicals, ingredients and additives that overload the body with toxins, weaken and disrupt our kids immune system and have been tied to hyperactivity, ADHD and cancer.

"*Simple Mills*" pumpkin and chocolate muffins

This gluten free, non-gmo formula is made with almond and coconut flour with minimal clean and wholesome ingredients. There are no artificial ingredients of any kind, so this is one of my top recommended brands for muffins, crackers, cookies, etc.

"*Flax 4 Life*" gluten free flax seed brownies

A perfect mini dessert for when you want something sweet and with chocolate! Most brownie mixes off the grocery shelves are made with ingredients like high fructose corn syrup, or hydrogenated oils that are toxic and create inflammation within the body once digested. Why not try a dairy free, gluten free brownie that contains clean ingredients, while also adding in the benefits of omega 3's by including flax seed within the ingredients? These brownie bites are a much better option to choose for our kids when they want an afternoon snack or something sweet. They are moist, delicious and come in perfect small muffin sizes.

ADDITIONAL SNACK OPTIONS

"Chomperz" seaweed chips

Yes, this snack recommendation may look and sound funny...but these little salty snacks can sneak in some major nutrients that are lacking in our everyday diets. Seaweed is much more dense than any land vegetable, as it contains micro-nutrients like folate, calcium, magnesium, zinc, iron, selenium, and omega 3 fatty acids DHA and EPA. Chomperz are a great way to get seaweed into your kids diet, while looking and tasting like a chip. You can choose original or BBQ flavor.

TIP: Iodine
Seaweed contains a great amount of iodine, which most of us as Americans are deficient in or at least low on. We need iodine to make thyroid hormones which control the body's metabolism, and also aids in bone and brain development during pregnancy and infancy.

"Peas please by Peeled Snacks" organic snacks

These yummy organic and non gmo snacks are very comparable to the "veggie straws" you see in the grocery store. This snack however contains cleaner organic ingredients while packing in 5 grams of protein with 1/2 a cup of veggies per serving! They are a great crunchy snack that could be a substitute for traditional chips that may not contain any nutritional value at all.

*Look for these at locations like Sprouts, Whole Foods, Publix, Safeway and Target.

"Emmy's Organics" coconut cookies

Organic, grain free and gluten free coconut peanut butter cookies for the win! These small cookies are a perfect thing to add to school lunches as they are small, super good and are made with nutritious ingredients. They come in numerous flavors so your kids have a variety in what they prefer, but our family's favorites are the peanut butter and dark chocolate cacao cookies!

"Simple Mills" Farmhouse cheddar crackers

Think of these as the healthier alternative to the popular "Cheez-it" crackers. These almond based crackers are paleo friendly, soy and corn free and have the cleanest ingredients like: Paprika and rosemary extract, cassava, organic cheddar cheese, sea salt, organic onion and garlic, tapioca, etc. Chunk the "Cheez-its" and give these crackers a try!

"Made in Nature" figgy pops

These organic bite-sized balls are made with fruits, nuts, seeds and spices that make a great energy-packed snack. They come in numerous flavor options like: mocha almond nut butter, apricot cashew nut butter, mango-berry and more. Figgy pops can be found at most health food grocery stores.

"Nada Moo" organic dairy-free ice cream

"Nada Moo" organic dairy-free ice cream is one of my most recent finds when on the hunt for a yummy, dairy-free and clean ingredient ice cream. There are a lot of dairy-free ice creams out there but they either taste like cardboard, or add in a bunch of ingredients like gums, thickeners, and syrups that are actually more toxic to the body when trying to stay away from cow dairy.

This brand is made with certified organic coconut milk, is 100% plant based, includes clean non-gmo ingredients, and has a super good creamy texture that actually tastes amazing!

I'm telling you, this dairy-free ice cream is my #1 pick due to how good it is, it tastes just the way a good creamy ice cream should taste.

*TIP: There are a few flavors in this brand that contain some ingredients I would NOT approve of, so here is the list that we buy:

- VANILLA..AHHH
- PISTACHIO NUT
- LOTTA MINT CHIP
- CREAMY COCONUT
- JAVA CRUNCH
- DUTCH CHOCOLATE

- CHOCOLATE PEANUT BUTTER
- MMM..MAPLE PECAN
- CHOCOLATE ALMOND CHIP
- HIMALAYAN SALTED CARAMEL
- CHOCOLATE CHERRY FUDGE BROWNIE

HEALTHY EATING ON THE GO

HEALTHY EATING ON THE GO

Maybe you are like me and simply would prefer to grab dinner on the way home from a busy day. Maybe you are like me and feel exhausted at the end of a long day at home with a baby or toddler? Maybe you work late, have a long commute drive home, or even teach classes like I do in the evenings. Whatever the end of your day looks like, sometimes to-go food or grabbing dinner while out and about is the easiest and most convenient thing to do.

While we want to keep life simple, easy and flowing smoothly with our schedules, I believe that somehow in our society convenience has led us down a path of neglecting the importance of health and wellness.

We have all been there....the early evening soccer practice, baseball game, dance class or instrument lesson that fills up our schedule each week. We as parents can end up feeling like glorified taxi drivers just getting each child to their destination at the correct times. The biggest obstacle many parents face is figuring out how to get a decent dinner into their kids' bellies before practice or the game begins, and this is usually where the drive-through comes in. Our family lives are busy these days. We rush from one place to the next and some families never experience one night together around the dinner table. There are seasons for every family where grab and go meals are simply what works for that particular season. We should be able to have plenty of good, quality options of places to go to get a healthy meal when on the go.

The reality is we need help with what places offer better ingredients, wiser choices from the menu that provide true nutrition with decent prices that serve it up quickly. This is where I hope to step in and suggest a few restaurants that will provide healthier on-the-go meals for busy families.

*I have included a few tips and tricks of how to choose wisely when ordering, and what places have better "kid" menus that provide real nutrition, not just frozen and fried food. have also listed a few examples of what we personally order for our son at a few of the selections of restaurants.

RECOMMENDED TIPS FOR EVERY LOCATION:

- Fill plate with bright colors, and avoid an abundance of white and brown foods.

- Skip out on added sugar in sweets (cookies, cake, candy, etc.).

- Leave out mayo, cheese & extra sauces.

- Fruits & veggies over fries and chips.

- Grilled over fried or breaded.

- Avoid dressings that contain canola oil, high fructose corn syrup, artificial colors, dyes and flavors. Choose balsamic vinegar and olive oil instead.

- Choose complex carbs, not the white processed refined breads & pastries.

MY FAVORITE NATIONAL RESTAURANTS:

SALATA SALAD BAR

Lots of variety to choose healthy options, but skip out on the salad dressings (most are canola oil based, so choose their balsamic vinegar and olive oil instead).

TAZIKI'S MEDITERRANEAN CAFE

Our pick - any of the kid meals, except grilled cheese. Choose fruit over chips.

WHOLE FOODS MARKET

Lots of variety to choose healthy options of the 5 food group focus in their hot bar or salad bar.

HEALTHY EATING ON THE GO

PEI WEI ASIAN DINER

Our pick - Kids honey-seared chicken, with brown rice and veggies.

ZOE'S KITCHEN

Our pick - Kids shrimp or salmon kabobs, chicken salad sandwich or grilled chicken fingers. Suggested sides are beans, veggies or hummus.

SCHLOTZSKY'S

Our pick - Kids chicken or kids turkey sandwich.

CHICK-FIL-A

Our pick - Grilled chicken nuggets, side of fruit.

CHIPOTLE MEXICAN GRILL

Our picks -
1.) Small brown rice bowl, pinto and black beans, grilled peppers, guacamole and tomatoes.
2.) Kids veggie quesadilla - black beans, brown rice, grilled peppers and very light on cheese, guacamole on top.

QDOBA MEXICAN GRILL

Our picks - Same meals as Chipotle.

PANERA BREAD

Our picks -
1.) Kids turkey sandwich, add mustard, leave off cheese.
2.) BBQ chicken flatbread sandwich, no cheese.
3.) Any of the 1/2 portion salads, our sons favorite is the Modern Greek with quinoa salad, or the Fuji apple chicken salad.

131

**THE FIVE FOOD GROUPS
TO FOCUS ON NO MATTER
WHERE YOU AND YOUR
FAMILY DINE OUT:**

Veggies

Protein

Complex Carbohydrate

Fruit

Healthy Fat

MY FAVORITE LOCAL CHOICES:

The following is a list of local restaurants that have a better option for kids meals that are either in the Edmond or Oklahoma City metropolitan area.

SATURN GRILL

Our picks - 1.) Kids roasted chicken breast meal with side of fruit
2.) Kids roasted wild salmon meal with side of fruit

THE REAL CAFE

Our pick - Kids grass-fed frank or burger meal with side of veggies

COOL GREENS

Our picks - 1.) Kids tasting plate
2.) Kids Skinny Florentine flatbread meal
3.) Kids Skinny BBQ flatbread meal
4.) Any kids salad
5.) California quinoa bowl

WHISKEY CAKES

Our pick - Sharing what my husband and I order and giving in smaller amounts to our son. Try the salmon, any of their salads and even a side dish off their farm to table menu.

ORGANIC SQUEEZE (smoothies & bowls)

You can't go wrong with any of the smoothies and bowls listed on menu.

Our son's favorites - 1.) CB & J
2.) Muscle Westbrook
3.) Tropical C
4.) Green Giant

CAFE ICON

Our pick - grilled chicken, steamed or fried rice, and edamame beans.

PROVISION KITCHEN

Highest quality local and organic ingredient dishes made to be easy to pick up and head home. There are numerous options of delicious foods to order from their hot bar when on the go.

NEIGHBORHOOD JAM

Our picks - 1.) Oats & Hay
2.) Acai bowl
3.) Avocado toast
4.) A side of eggs, avocado and turkey sausage, with their Power Greens smoothie.

CAFE 501

Our picks - 1.) Oven roasted turkey sandwich with side of fruit for lunch.
2.) Kids scrambled eggs meal for brunch.

HOLEY ROLLERS
(better alternative donuts)

Clean ingredient donuts made 100% dairy free, egg free and some gluten free options as well. If you are going to get a donut, this is the place to go to eat better quality hand crafted sweets.

Check out these local farms if you are in the Edmond or Oklahoma City metro area:

BF FARMS - (bf-farms.com)

OKLAHOMA FOOD COOPERATIVE (shop.oklahomafood.coop)

PROVIDENCE FARMS - (Edmond, OK) on Facebook

133

HEALTHY HYDRATION

HEALTHY HYDRATION

My husband and I have started routinely using the same phrase each day with our son when we know it's time for him to drink more water. We fill up his cup, twist on the lid and say, "Here buddy, time to hydrate up!" I don't know when that began, but the phrase works as he takes the cup out of our hands and begins taking big gulps.

We use the "Berkey" water filter in our home for drinking water. We also buy bags of organic frozen fruit to put a few pieces into his cup as a way to keep things fun and to give natural, pure flavor to the water.

Staying hydrated is so crucial for our little ones, but how we do it can either be beneficial or harmful depending on what it is that we make routine for what our kids drink each day. Soda, juice boxes made with artificial ingredients, and even carton milk or Yoohoo chocolate milk have become so normal that most days they wont even get the necessary amount of water needed to stay hydrated.

We need to get back to the basics of making water the primary source of what kids drink. Large food and beverage companies heavily market their products without concern for our health. We have to recognize we are creating sugar addicts by pumping our kids full of artificial dyes and toxic chemicals. We have given in to the notion that these drinks do not cause long-term harm.

Here are some healthy hydration options that not only will ensure your kids stay hydrated, but will also provide electrolytes, less added sugar and options to choose better ingredients.

TIPS:

* Water should be the main source of how we hydrate our kids. Fill it with organic fresh or frozen fruits and herbs.

* Avoid drinks like Gatorade & Powerade that are filled with sugar, artificial flavors, modified corn starch, and artificial colors/dyes that are linked to hyperactivity, cancer, & allergic reactions.

* Avoid juice boxes that are filled with added sugars and artificial colors/flavors that do not provide any nutritional value.

FROZEN FRUIT AND HERB WATER

Water should be the primary source of fluids we give our children. It's what keeps our organs, tissue and muscles hydrated. An infants body is typically made up of around 75% water, while the average adult body averages about 60% make up of water.

We need to ensure that the majority of what we drink in a day is water, and not sugary substitutes.

GREAT COMBOS TO TRY:

- **Cucumber Mint**
- **Watermelon Basil**
- **Strawberry, Lemon, Lime**
- **Pineapple Basil**
- **Cantaloupe, Blueberry, Mint**
- **Raspberry Rosemary**
- **Lime, Lemon, Pink Himalayan Sea Salt (just a pinch)**

MY FAVORITE HEALTHY DRINKS

"Drink Maple" **maple water**

Maple water provides natural electrolytes & gives a sweet hint of flavor. Contains less sugar than coconut water, and comes in a variety of flavors or original maple.

"Leaf and Love" organic lemonade

Juice boxes made with organic and non-gmo ingredients that taste like homemade lemonade! No artificial ingredients, no sugar alcohols, and sweetened only with lemon and stevia plant extracts. An added bonus of pink himalayan sea salt that provides healthy hydration and aids the adrenal glands.

"Wonder-Well" organic water

These organic "water" boxes are lightly sweetened with natural fruits and no artificial sweeteners or sugar. What a great option to provide a more natural approach to giving our kids something sweet but focusing primarily on water.

"Spindrift" sparkling water

Spindrift is the first sparkling water made with only real squeezed fruit. It is colorful just like the real fruit it contains, and it does NOT contain any "natural flavors" that can actually contain up to 100 unknown ingredients within the term that most other food and drink companies include in their products.

"Nuun" electrolyte hydration tabs

Drop these tabs into water to provide essential hydration and essential electrolytes like sodium, potassium, magnesium & calcium that are lost in exercise, sweat & summer heat. A great alternative to Gatorade, Powerade or other sports drinks that use color dyes, added sugars and corn syrup.

"Bossi" organic tea for kids

The new alternative box drink for kids that I hope begins to start a new trend or the "norm" of drink boxes! For sports activities, school lunch boxes, kids parties, and special events. Organic, caffeine-free rooibos tea for kids! No artificial ingredients or juice. These kid teas come in yummy flavors & are a great healthy option to a "box" drink.

HOMEMADE ELECTROLYTE DRINK

This is a seriously delicious recipe to whip up for an all-natural electrolyte drink without the artificial dyes, flavors, and added sugars that are included in popular drinks like Gatorade. Electrolytes are essential to the body and are made up of: Sodium, Potassium, Magnesium, Calcium, Chloride and Phosphorus, which help balance fluid pressure inside our cells and control the pH in our blood.

The following recipe is filled with electrolytes and would be a great option to make in bulk and store in the refrigerator.

- **1 cup organic coconut water**
- **1/2 cup pineapple juice**
- **1/2 cup orange juice**
- **1-2 teaspoons of raw local honey or "Manuka" honey**
- **2 pinches of pink himalayan sea salt**
- **1/2 fresh squeezed lime**
- **1/2 fresh squeezed lemon**

Mix all together in a large pitcher and add ice!

MORE OF MY FAVORITE HEALTHY DRINKS

"Izze" organic sparkling flavored water

Organic sparkling water drinks that come in many yummy flavors with minimal ingredients like: Carbonated water, organic cane sugar (1 g), citric acid and * organic natural flavors.

(*Natural flavors are unfortunately everywhere in our food and drink products. They can technically contain up to 100 unknown ingredients within the term. I will recommend these drinks ONLY because they have "organic" natural flavors, which will be a better choice than non-organic).

HEALTHY HYDRATION

"Zevia" sparkling water

Another option I will recommend that are better alternatives to soda is Zevia sparkling water. Zevia contains cleaner ingredients than the traditional sodas that I would not recommend at all due to artificial colors, flavors, preservatives, high fructose corn syrups (toxic, artificial and a genetically modified ingredient) and large amounts of sugar, or toxic artificial sweeteners like Aspartame and Sucralose.

Zevia is a non-gmo drink, without caramel coloring, phosphoric acid (which is harmful to bones, teeth and kidneys) and is sweetened with stevia leaf and real ingredients like citrus oil and ginger.

'R.W. Knudsen" organic juice

This organic, gluten free, non-gmo juice box brand contains quality ingredients of: filtered water, natural juices, no added sugar, colors or other artificial ingredients. Contains 100% real juice, with clean minimal ingredients.

Option to buy juice boxes, or purchase the "Simply Nutritious" blends in large glass containers like our family does for when we want something sweet to add to our morning or in smoothies! Our favorites are: "Mega Green," "Morning Blend," and "Mega C."

'Coconut Water" Water with a purpose!

Coconut water is a natural electrolyte replacement & contains more potassium than a banana! You can choose the regular creamy coconut water, or sparkling coconut water option as well!

Always choose an organic brand

139

"Ella's Kitchen" organic super strawberry lemonade with Aloe Vera

I love this organic juice box for its clean ingredients, low sugar grams, with no artificial colors, flavors, preservatives or GMO's. However, what I love most about this juice box is an added ingredient that you don't see in other juice box brands... Aloe Vera!

Aloe Vera is incredibly soothing to the digestive tract due to its anti-inflammatory and laxative components. It helps with digestion, encourages digestive good bacteria, normalizes acid/alkaline pH balance and helps prevent constipation. Aloe Vera is a very smart ingredient to include in a juice when you do choose to pick a juice box for your little one over the age of 1 year old.

"Honest Kids" organic juice

This is also a better option than most other name brand juice boxes, as the ingredients are clean and it contains lower sugar as well. This juice is organic, non-gmo and gluten free and comes in a variety of flavors that kids love. It does contain "organic natural flavors" which is better than regular added "natural flavors," so just be mindful of how many things your little one is consuming that contains "natural flavors" each day.

(*Natural flavors are unfortunately everywhere in our food and drink products. They can technically contain up to 100 unknown ingredients within the term.)

"Hydrate by Beachbody" electrolyte citrus powder

An entire tub of natural electrolytes that can be used in water bottles at the ballpark, beach or lake for months on end. No artificial ingredients (flavors, dyes or sugars) of any kind with a subtle citrus flavor.

This is a great option when you need electrolyte replacement options in bulk for the entire family. One scoop per 8-12 oz of water gives all the potassium, magnesium, sodium and calcium needed to replace what is lost through sweat, sports and summer activities.

*This can be purchased online or directly through my personal link:
https://mysite.coach.teambeachbody.com/?coachId=958219&locale=en_US

HEALTHY HYDRATION

AXLE'S "FIZZY BERRY LIMEADE"

Our son loves when we mix this up for him because he says it tastes like a "fizzy berry limeade!"

A drink I feel good about the ingredients when he wants something fun to drink without the added sugars, artificial dyes and corn syrups that other juice blends contain.

Recipe:

The Mountain Valley" lime sparkling water (can use perrier or pelligrino)

R.W. Knudsen's organic "Just Cranberry" all natural juice

1/2-1 fresh squeezed lime juice

Mix all together and you have a drink that provides fizz, tartness and sweetness without all the added sugar and junk ingredients!

141

IMMUNE SUPPORT

IMMUNE SUPPORT

I am 100% "that" wife and mom that prepares vitamins and supplements the night before for my husband and son. I pack up a weekly vitamin container with all the essentials for my husband to take with him when he travels, and I without hesitation will pack up all my sons supplements with written directions and send them in his bag when he goes to stay with his grandparents. While it may seem silly to some, it's really just become a part of our everyday life to remain healthy and keep the immune system boosted. It's like brushing our teeth or showering ... we incorporate vitamins, minerals and herbs into our life, not necessarily as a means to treat anything at the time, but more so to practice prevention and healthy living protocols.

I firmly believe the best way to keep our children healthy and to prevent sickness is to boost the immune system naturally through healthy clean food, plenty of filtered water, eliminating toxins from their body and environment, ensuring they get adequate quality sleep, and by taking some natural immune-boosting supplements. As a Certified Holistic Nutritionist, I can't give any kind of medical advice but I can give examples of what we use in our home and list recommendations of supplement brands that I have researched and believe have the upmost quality and standards. My focus is nutrition and helping other parents gain the knowledge as to what that is and how to achieve it for their families. However, like many things in life, I believe we have to look at a puzzle as a whole and not focus on just one piece. I feel the best kind of nutrition is a combination of things like whole and raw foods, mixed with natural supplements in a synergistic manner to create and maintain the strongest immune system that can kick anything that gets in its way.

Here are some supplements that we give our son either daily, intermittently or when we can tell he might need a boost upon sickness.

BLACK ELDERBERRY SYRUP

"Gaia for Kids" Black elderberry syrup

Elderberry is the most powerful natural anti-viral fighter that also acts as a diuretic, which opens the blood vessels to help lower a fever naturally. It boosts the immune system, and it's one of the first things we give our son if we can see he might be getting sick. The dose is based on age of child and is listed clearly on the back of the label. This is a great supplement to use during flu season or even for normal viruses and illnesses when the first sign of illness presents itself. Elderberry is also used for other symptoms and ailments like: sciatica and chronic fatigue syndrome.

*Take as a seasonal preventative during back to school time, holidays or large gathering at events, first sign of virus, (especially flu) or during sickness.

"Sambucus Immune" Black elderberry syrup

This formula is another great way to boost your child's immune system with a full-spectrum black elderberry extract, Vitamin C, Zinc and Echinacea. This combination is a brilliant mixture of important nutrients and vitamins to support a full coverage of boosting the immune system to work in the way its supposed to.

This is a product we will give to our son if he has been around other sick children, or if traveling in sick season or early onset of illness. We boost with a daily dosage a few days past event, or until illness is over.

VITAMIN D3

"Springboard Kid-D Liquid Drops" by Ortho Molecular Products

Specially formulated for children under 100lbs and looking to get all the benefits of vitamin d through a safe, child-formulated supplement. If your child suffers from poor immunity, slow growth, metabolic issues, childhood illnesses, low mood or poor focus, supplementing with a quality vitamin d product could help benefit your child greatly.

*Since many children routinely test out of the optimal range for healthy level of vitamin D, its suggested to supplement with approximately 35IU's per pound of body weight.

IMMUNE SUPPORT

"*Child Life*" Organic Vitamin D3

Healthy levels of Vitamin D3 are essential to a healthy immune system. It regulates antimicrobial proteins and is critical to immune response in defending against viruses, pathogens and bacteria. Deficiency in Vitamin D3 can be linked to many autoimmune disorders, asthma, autism and other neurological conditions.

Vitamin D3 is actually a hormone produced when the sun is exposed to our skin, then turning into Vitamin D3 once absorbed into the body. Contrary to synthetic Vitamin D2 (fortified and added to our foods/drinks), Vitamin D3 is natural & essential.

Boost especially during winter months when sun exposure is low. When your shadow is longer than you are tall, the sunshine you are receiving is not producing Vitamin D and supplementation is needed. Depending on where you live, it may be best to supplement in months between October and March.

*Lab testing is best to find out what level you or your child is at. Ask for a Vitamin D3 test and see where you need to be in "optimal" range, not just "normal" range. Optimal ranges in the 25-hydroxyvitamin D test should be between 50-70 ng/ml.

**The rule of thumb for dosing is: 35IU's (drops are measured in IU=international units) per pound of body weight.

DAILY NUTRITION DRINK

"*Equilibrium Nutrition*" Daily fruit and vegetable blend mix, Dr. Stephen Cabral

Need a little help getting your young ones to get the necessary daily dose of fruits and greens each day?

This 22 organic vegetable, fruit and berry mix is brightly colored and non-oxidized, as the powders are protected from heat, UV light and moisture. These greens have a paleo profile, contain NO grains, legumes, alfalfa, corn, gluten, fructose or artificial sweeteners.

There are NO fillers, bulking agents, pectin, rice bran or other ingredients that can account for up to 60% of the content in other greens products.

Instantly mixes in water without blending and makes water a super bright and on green color! **This is unsweetened so my best recommendation is to add it to smoothie!

IMMUNE SUPPORT

"Garden of Life" Dr. Formulated Probiotics + Vitamin C & D3, Organic Kids

5 billion organisms, 14 probiotic strains plus an added dose of Vitamin C and Vitamin D3! This brand is organic, non-gmo, gluten, dairy, and soy free and also contains a prebiotic blend of organic acacia fiber and cranberry!

"Springboard Floraboost Probiotics" by Ortho Molecular Products

Helps maintain gastrointestinal balance, increases secretory IGA for enhanced gut immunity, supports bowel regularity, supports digestion and micronutrient absorption.

"Child Life" Probiotics with Colostrum

This probiotic combines 3 highly potent ingredients for a strong approach to health for children. Probiotic blend is the ideal balance to support healthy intestinal function. Colostrum is added to provide a full spectrum of immune factors and boosters. Prebiotics support the growth of probiotics to maintain healthy digestion and immune function. There are no artificial ingredients, gmo's, alcohol, gluten or soy.

*May be used for ongoing maintenance for children 2 years and older.

"Meta Kids Probiotics" by Metagenics

A proprietary blend of highly viable, pure strains of friendly bacteria that supports immune health. Natural grape flavored chewable formula is backed by the Metagenics ID guarantee for purity, clinical reliability and safety.

"Florajen 4 Kids" Probiotics

This is an important gut health protection that I believe every child should be getting in their diet. Our current food and medical system produces so many synthetic, processed and toxic ingredients that are put into the foods we eat and the medicines that are taken, that we are damaging the natural gut flora and good bacteria on a daily basis.

Probiotics help build the good bacteria and gut lining to support a vital role in our immune health. Think of the gut as the second brain of the body. If it's not functioning properly it can be extremely detrimental to overall health and wellness within the body.

Foods high in probiotics can be found in yogurt (see my recommended brands in the grocery list), kombucha drinks, and fermented foods like : raw sauerkraut, kefir, kimchi, and pickles.

VITAMIN C

"Child Life" Liquid Vitamin C

This natural orange liquid formula contains no artificial ingredients, dairy, soy, gluten, gmo's or alcohol. It's a clean and pure product and a great way to boost a child's immune system.

Follow instructions on back of label for dosage.

"Metagenics" Ultra potent-C powder

Making sure your child gets the proper amount of daily Vitamin C is important, and should first come through food sources like: red peppers, oranges, papaya, strawberries, broccoli, dark leafy greens and citrus fruits. However, if you need a supplement to help boost Vitamin C when these foods are not being consumed, this would be a quality brand and powder to consider.

Ultra Potent-C" powder may help support healthy immune function and is a good source of antioxidants from vitamin C. Contains L-Glutathione, which is an important antioxidant. This powder may improve uptake of the vitamin by white blood cells when compared to regular ascorbic acid.

Follow instructions on back of label for dosage

"Gaia Kids" Bronchial Wellness

Natural support for children's throat and bronchial health. This formula is organic and use herbs like plantain and grindelia, which are used to promote respiratory health and is naturally processed to ensure high concentration and absorption. Kids will love the flavor as it comes from organic honey and essential oils. This product contains no artificial ingredients of any kind.

We will boost our sons immune system with this product in fall or winter when/if he begins to come down with a cold, cough or early onset of an illness.

*Follow instructions on back of label

"Traditional Medicinals Just for Kids" Kids Cold Care herbal tea

Organic non-caffeine herbal tea made with mild peppermint, chamomile and herbs like elder flower in child-size amounts. Great for when kids come down with the sniffles, sneezing or when typical winter cold symptoms begin to appear.

*For children 2 and up, suggested amount listed on label for each age.

"Kid's Xlear" Natural saline nasal spray with Xylitol

This all natural saline spray promotes upper respiratory health by cleansing and moisturizing the nasal passages. The patented solution with xylitol helps wash away airborne contaminants and pollutants, but also can help reduce infections by reducing the ability of harmful bacteria, pollens, allergens and other irritants from adhering to nasal tissue.

*We spray this solution into our son's nose and then use the "NoseFrida" to suck any additional mucus out of his sinuses. The Xlear spray helps moisturize and prepare the nose to loosen mucus to come out more easily

IMMUNE SUPPORT

OMEGA SUPPORT

"Nordic Naturals" Baby's DHA (plus vitamin d3)

1050 mg of Omega 3 PLUS 300 IU vitamin D3 drops support infant brain, nervous system and visual development for babies between 5-35lbs.

*See recommended dosing and clearly marked dropper for easy measuring.

"OmegAvail Lemon Drop Smoothie" Omega 3 liquid drops

This is a great emulsified Omega 3 option that contains important EPA and DHA that tastes like lemon drops! EPA and DHA are essential for brain and eye health, as well as keeping a good balance to offset the amounts of high Omega 6's that come in a lot of our processed foods and cooking oils that can create inflammation and toxic buildup in the body over time. This is my top health recommendation for an omega 3 supplement as it does not contain added sugars that some of the "gummy" omega 3 supplements add in. These lemon drops make a great "lemon" smoothie, so you can experiment with how you use them!

*Can be used daily or intermittently

"Nordic Naturals" Omega 3 fatty acid gummy

Omega EPA & DHA is crucial to brain and eye health. This fatty acid is important for kids of 2 years and older and can be given through a fun gummy by Nordic Naturals in many different shapes like fish, berries, or gummy worms. They do not contain any artificial colors, flavors, preservatives or ingredients of any kind.

These gummies do contain 3-4 grams of organic sugar and organic tapioca syrup, which some parents may not feel comfortable with since it would be adding in extra sugar to a daily supplement. So, the gummy would be my last choice to use if the liquid omega drops were not an option, or if you have a child who will not consume the liquid version.

Can be used daily or intermittently, at 2 years of age or older.

"Thorne, Children's Basic Nutrients" Multivitamin

This multivitamin offers comprehensive vitamin & mineral supplementation for kids 4 and up, however...they do have directions on how to dose ages 1 year and up on label as well.

"Metagenics, PhytoMulti" Multivitamin

Do not neglect the importance of getting minerals and vitamins from clean, organic whole foods as a main source for nutrients in your child's diet. Second to that, there is an option for a multi vitamin for children 4 years and older that contains Phytonutrients with 9 fruit and vegetable powders.

*Can be taken daily for ages 4 and older only.

"Smarty Pants" Non Gmo Kids multivitamin

This gummy multivitamin with fiber is actually sold at local health food stores if you want something to pick up while grocery shopping. The reason I like this vitamin is due to its quality ingredients, minerals and vitamins. It contains the correct and appropriate type of methylated Vitamin B12, Methylcobalamin. It contains Vitamin D3, Omega 3 fish oil, Niacin, Iodine (which a majority of us are very deficient in), and it also contains the correct methylated form of Folate, Methylfolate. All essential nutrients for our growing kids in the correct form that is better digested and more easily absorbed.

*For kids 3 years of age and older

"Equilibrium Nutrition" Daily activated multivitamin

A comprehensive, hypo-allergenic, multi-vitamin and mineral blend that provides high-quality nutrients to build a healthy micronutrient reserve. Contains pure forms of methylated vitamins and the biologically active form of folate, instead of the synthetic version of folic acid.

*Can be taken for children 4 years and older.

ILLNESS PROTOCOL

"Immune FX, RXFX" Immunoglobulin capsules or powder

A dairy free, natural source of bovine serum-derived immunoglobulin antibodies & immunoproteins that provide immune support to boost the gut and fight against bacteria, viruses and fungus. It boosts immunoglobulin levels within the GI tract, reduces gut inflammation and lessens gut permeability. It can bind and neutralize major pathogens like H Pylori and contains beneficial immune-regulating cytokines (important for cell function and signaling).

We use these capsules or powder when we want to boost the immune system, or at the first sign of sickness and then continue through until well. I also give it to my son to supplement with if traveling on a plane or around large amount of people for an event. I will usually give it to him the day of event, or travel and end a few days after returning home. You have a choice of the capsule, or simply sprinkle the powder version onto yogurt, applesauce, cereal or any cold food for your child.

*Can be taken intermittently as a proactive booster, or at first sign of illness. We have always used 1 teaspoon in early ages, up to 1 tablespoon now as a 3 year old.

"Vital Nutrients" Arabinogalactan powder

This is a great prebiotic supplement that is derived from sugar made from the bark of larch trees. It enhances natural killer cell activity, which is very important not only for kids but in adults as well. This powder is a natural digestive aid that supports healthy microflora in the gut, and is also an immune boosting fiber supplement that also has antimicrobial effects.

*I give our son 1/2 a teaspoon in his water each week to keep his gut flora and immune system strong.

"Boiron" Oscillococcinum

One of the best all-around homeopathic sickness prevention tools we keep on hand!
Oscillococcinum can be found almost anywhere now, so simply look for it at your local grocery store, pharmacy, online or even some retail stores. This is great for flu-like symptoms, fever, chills, body aches or simply feeling run down. This is best to start at the first sign of illness or flu for it to effectively work.

We dose by giving 1 vial (1 vial= 1 dose) 3 times over a 24 hour period. This dose can be for adults AND kids.

PURE FOOD PROJECT
FOR KIDS!

[RESOURCES]

PRODUCT RESOURCES

WHERE I SHOP:

For all of the food and drink items listed within my book, I shop primarily at health food grocery stores like: Sprouts, Natural Grocers and Whole Foods. I'm sure other grocery stores will carry some of the brands throughout the book, but those are my go-to grocery stores when I shop local.

For brands that are not found at your local grocery store, you can search on Amazon.com or thrivemarket.com and have them shipped to your house! This is where you can find a lot of my favorite snack and healthy hydration recommendations. For the immune support supplements, please reference to the company website, Amazon.com or simply check your local health food grocery store shelves.

If you use my Thrive Market link below, you will receive 25% off of your first order!

http://thrv.me/lindsayamilianholisticnutritionist

COOKWARE:

The best non-toxic cookware materials are ceramic, stainless steel, cast iron and glass. Using non-stick traditional teflon cookware is highly toxic due to the dangerous levels of PFOA, lead, and PFAS that seep into food and inhaled when cooking. Green pan ceramic cookware is naturally a non-stick surface and is a clean, non-toxic cookware to use for daily cooking.

Website: greenpan.us

HIGH POWER BLENDER:

We use our Vitamix almost everyday making smoothies for breakfast, or for a yummy snack. The Vitmamix grinds up even the tiniest bits of spinach or seeds, so we prefer it over others as it makes the smoothie texture completely smooth and creamy.

Websites : vitamix.com or Amazon

GLASS FOOD STORAGE CONTAINERS:

Using glass storage containers is a non-toxic way to store food in the refrigerator, as opposed to using plastic which can contain BPA, lead, and other toxic materials used in the making of plastic. Adding your hot leftovers to plastic containers can actually warm up the plastic, allowing small amounts of plastic to inevitably get into food. Find a selection of different sizes of containers with coordinating lids.

Websites : You can search any company or brand you choose on Amazon, Target or Bed Bath and Beyond.

"IF YOU CARE" PARCHMENT BAKING PAPER

Instead of cooking or warming up food with foil, we use a FSC and compostable certified unbleached and chlorine free parchment paper in our toaster oven or conventional oven. It's a more natural and safe approach to warming foods and can be bought at your local health food grocery store.

May be purchased at Sprouts, Target, Amazon, Walmart or thrivemarket.com

DIVIDED PLATES:

We use colored kid divider plates that are made from recycled milk jugs and are BPA, PVC, and Phthalate free!

Websites : re-play.com

LUNCHBOXES:

"LunchBots" stainless steel food containers make great lunchboxes for kids when you need a non-toxic material container with dividers for food. Eco-friendly, dishwasher safe and BPA-free!

Website: lunchbots.com

NONTOXIC BAMBOO TABLEWARE:

Avanchy provides organic bamboo and stainless steel plates, bowls, and utensils for babies and kids. Non toxic materials like bamboo and stainless steel are better alternatives to plastic due to high levels of BPA, BPS, PVC, lead and toxic Phthalate materials.

Website: avanchy.com

"Planetbox" stainless steel and certified non toxic lunchboxes are perfect for those who want more variety with sizes and compartments to hold food. They have a variety of models that each come with different dipping containers and dividers!

Website: planetbox.com

"Bentgo" leak-proof kids on the go lunchboxes are another great option when you want numerous dividers and containers to pack your kids food for the day. Contains removable compartment trays and comes in a variety of fun colors to choose from.

Website: bentgo.com

Bella Tunno has adorable multi-colored suction plates that are 100% food-grade silicone and BPA and PVC free. They are dishwasher safe and perfect for portion size with their dividers. For every product sold, they donate 1 meal to a child in America!

Websites : bellatunno.com

GLASS WATER BOTTLES/TUMBLERS:

Whether its a baby bottle, toddler sippy cup or adult water bottle...glass is a clean material to be using day in and day out for a drink bottle. Ello provides a variety of colorful silicone sleeves that wrap around the bottle to prevent shattering they if they fall on the ground and are the perfect way to cradle the cups and provide a healthier route to get those ounces of water in each day!

Websites : elloproducts.com or Amazon.com

WATER FILTRATION SYSTEM:

To purify our drinking water, we use a Berkey purification system in our home. It is highly rated and filters out more harmful chemicals and pollutants than the standard filters sold at stores. It removes viruses, cysts, parasites, pathogenic bacteria, fluoride, and heavy metals like mercury and lead that can be found in our local tap water sources.

Websites : berkeyfilters.com or Amazon

RESOURCES

GLASS SMOOTHIE JARS WITH LID AND STRAW

We use these eco friendly, non toxic mason jars for all smoothie blends. Using glass, ceramic, or stainless steel are better than using plastic due to high amounts of toxins, BPA, BPS, PVS and Phthalates used in the making of plastic. They also can be used as baby food storage containers as well.

Website: jervisandgeorge.com

SPICES: SIMPLY ORGANIC

We use numerous spices when cooking to add flavor to food, instead of additional sugar or sweeteners. We use "Simply Organic" spices on our eggs, meats, veggies and fish. Our staple spices include Cinnamon, Black pepper, Pink himalayan sea salt, Lemon pepper, Cumin, Thyme, Italian and All-purpose seasoning.

Website: simplyorganic.com

COOKING OILS:

- Organic and non-gmo coconut, avocado or grapeseed oil for high heat use.

- Organic and non-gmo coconut, avocado or olive oil for cold use.

CHOOSING WHICH FOODS SHOULD BE ORGANIC:

Follow the yearly "Dirty Dozen, Clean 15" list (you can simply google this list, as a new one is put out each year) to see which fruits and vegetables should always be purchased as organic, and which fruits and vegetables can be bought as non-organic.

*The Dirty Dozen app by Environmental Working Group is also available to download directly to your phone by selecting the " Dirty Dozen" inside your app store.

CHECKING SAFETY LEVELS IN FOOD & PRODUCTS:

The Environmental Working Group (EWG) has a great website (ewg.org) that provides a guide to safe and healthy products on the market for the consumer to check before purchasing. They rate items from food to furniture, to household and skincare products and more.

*You can also download the app directly to your phone, by selecting "EWG's Healthy Living," and the " EWG's Food Scores" app inside your app store.
Find out more here: https://www.ewg.org/videos/ewgs-healthy-living-app

RECOMMENDED DOCUMENTARIES:

These are a few short documentaries that are helpful and filled with great education when it comes to understanding the "WHY" behind my recommendations and suggestions within this book. This is a great way to include the entire family in on new health goals and bringing awareness to why changes need to take place and how attainable they truly can be!

- "Fed Up"
- "The Magic Pill"
- "GMOs Revealed"
- "Forks over Knives"

PURE FOOD PROJECT FOR KIDS! GROCERY LIST

I put together this quick list to help you get started on your PURE FOOD journey. Just tear this page out and you can take this resource with you! You can add your own items as you read through this book. Please see my complete Grocery List at the beginning of this book.

*REMEMBER: Fresh or frozen is better than canned, choose organic & Non-GMO, and have fun while considering your menu!

VEGETABLES

- ☐ Broccoli
- ☐ Peas
- ☐ Spinach
- ☐ Peppers
- ☐ _____
- ☐ _____
- ☐ _____

FRUITS

- ☐ Avocados
- ☐ Oranges
- ☐ Raspberries
- ☐ Blueberries
- ☐ _____
- ☐ _____
- ☐ _____

NUTS & SEEDS

- ☐ Almonds
- ☐ Walnuts
- ☐ Pumpkin Seeds
- ☐ Chia Seeds
- ☐ _____
- ☐ _____
- ☐ _____

COMPLEX CARBOHYDRATES

- ☐ Gluten Free Oatmeal
- ☐ Sprouted or Seed Bread
- ☐ Organic Pasta
- ☐ Quinoa
- ☐ Brown or Wild Rice
- ☐ Tortilla Wraps
- ☐ _____
- ☐ _____
- ☐ _____
- ☐ _____
- ☐ _____

DAIRY

- ☐ Non-Dairy Milk
- ☐ Ghee
- ☐ Yogurt
- ☐ Organic Cheese
- ☐ _____
- ☐ _____
- ☐ _____
- ☐ _____
- ☐ _____
- ☐ _____
- ☐ _____
- ☐ _____

PANTRY & SNACKS

- [ ] Gluten Free Crackers
- [ ] Snack Bars
- [ ] Granola
- [ ] Healthy Chips
- [ ] Cereals
- [ ] Popcorn
- [ ] Raw Honey
- [ ] Organic Ketchup
- [ ] Organic Maple Syrup
- [ ] _____
- [ ] _____
- [ ] _____
- [ ] _____
- [ ] _____
- [ ] _____
- [ ] _____
- [ ] _____

OTHER

- [ ] _____
- [ ] _____
- [ ] _____
- [ ] _____
- [ ] _____
- [ ] _____
- [ ] _____
- [ ] _____
- [ ] _____
- [ ] _____
- [ ] _____
- [ ] _____

PROTEIN

- [ ] Organic Nitrate-Free Chicken Sausage
- [ ] Turkey Deli Rollups
- [ ] Organic Grass-Fed Beef
- [ ] Organic Cage-Free, Free Range Eggs
- [ ] Frozen Veggie Burger Patties
- [ ] Black Beans
- [ ] _____
- [ ] _____
- [ ] _____
- [ ] _____

SPICES & OILS

- [ ] Organic Cinnamon
- [ ] Organic Black Pepper
- [ ] Organic Lemon Pepper Seasoning
- [ ] Pink Himalayan Sea Salt
- [ ] Unrefined Virgin Coconut Oil
- [ ] Organic Avocado Oil
- [ ] Organic Extra Virgin Olive Oil
- [ ] _____
- [ ] _____
- [ ] _____

SIDES

- [ ] Hummus
- [ ] Healthy Salad Dressings
- [ ] Nut Butter
- [ ] Plant-Based Protein Powder
- [ ] _____
- [ ] _____
- [ ] _____

PURE FOOD PROJECT FOR KIDS! SAMPLE MEAL PLAN

Putting together your Meal Plan is simple! This is just a sample Clean Eating Meal Plan that you can follow and room for you to create your own Meal Plan. All of my suggestions are listed in the book!

SUNDAY

BREAKFAST:	Paleo pancakes or gluten free waffle
LUNCH:	Sweet italian sausage with veggies & fruit
DINNER:	Shrimp & quinoa/millet mix

MONDAY

BREAKFAST:	Muffin and Eggs
LUNCH:	Almond toast & Hemp Heart yogurt
DINNER:	Wild caught salmon & ravioli

TUESDAY

BREAKFAST:	Oatmeal & nut bowl
LUNCH:	Turkey rollup
DINNER:	Spaghetti

WEDNESDAY

BREAKFAST:	Avocado mash toast
LUNCH:	Tuna salad
DINNER:	Burrito dinner

THURSDAY

BREAKFAST:	Peach cereal
LUNCH:	Chicken sausage & Avocado
DINNER:	Asparagus & sweet potatoes

FRIDAY

BREAKFAST:	Baked egg muffins
LUNCH:	Grilled cheese
DINNER:	Turkey & peppers

SATURDAY

BREAKFAST:	Overnight oat jar
LUNCH:	Leftover turkey loaf
DINNER:	Pizza & salad

**Substitute any "Lunchbox meals" for lunches, and use any "Smoothie" recipes for a snack or additional breakfast side.

MEAL PLAN

NOTES:

SUNDAY

BREAKFAST:

LUNCH:

DINNER:

MONDAY

BREAKFAST:

LUNCH:

DINNER:

TUESDAY

BREAKFAST:

LUNCH:

DINNER:

WEDNESDAY

BREAKFAST:

LUNCH:

DINNER:

THURSDAY

BREAKFAST:

LUNCH:

DINNER:

FRIDAY

BREAKFAST:

LUNCH:

DINNER:

SATURDAY

BREAKFAST:

LUNCH:

DINNER:

ACKNOWLEDGEMENTS

Knowledge is a powerful thing when we open ourselves up to apply it. There is so much to learn about nutrition, health and overall wellness of the body but you have to be willing to open your eyes and ears to embrace some truths that you may have never wanted to know, or come to know as truths. Change can be hard, and the realization of the need to change can be even harder.

Taking action and deciding to change the way you live your life is the #1 big step to take. Following through comes next, and staying consistent will help you achieve true change.

I am so grateful for the experiences in my life that have taught me what true health means, what real nutrition looks like, and most importantly for the courage to share with others when I saw a need.

Thank you to my local pharmacists at Innovative pharmacy in Edmond, OK for being willing to teach me about supplements more in depth, and for taking the time to explain how they work in conjunction with the body to help it heal and thrive.

Thank you to Dr. Stephen Cabral for being the incredible Naturopathic & Functional Medicine physician that you are, and for sharing free knowledge everyday on your podcast to help the world learn how to achieve true wellness and overcome sickness and disease. You have inspired me in numerous ways throughout my journey as a Holistic Nutritionist.

Thank you to the numerous influencial health practitioners that speak truth, share wisdom and help spread knowledge regarding natural health, functional medicine and a more holistic way of attaining wellness. A huge shout out to the following practitioners that I love learning from: Dr. Mark Hyman, Dr. David Perlmutter, Dr. Joseph Mercola, Dr. Ben Lynch, Dr. Paul Thomas, Dr. Elisa Song, Dr. Raphael Kellman, Dr. Suzanne Humphries, and many more.

Thank you to my graphic designer, Gina McKinnis for being the motivator that I have needed to pursue every project and new endeavor that I have began in the last few years. Not only are you super talented in your design, but you have the gift of encouragement and cheering me on to push past doubts and reach for big goals!

Thank you to every person who has joined me and been a part of my Pure Body Reset program online. I applaud you for your 4 week journey of taking the time to walk through the program I created. Thank you so much for your trust in me and for your willingness to change your life for the better!

Thank you to every member that attends my dance fitness classes at numerous locations in Edmond and the Oklahoma City area! You guys are rock stars and your dedication to my weekly classes inspires me and drives me forward as a fitness instructor. I'm so grateful for you all!

Thank you to my husband and my two boys, my parents, friends and family who constantly encourage me, and share my information on social media. You guys are the backbone that help support me and lift me up when I need affirmation and inspiration to share my passion and dreams with others.

Made in the USA
Monee, IL
26 July 2020

37020308R00100